RESUMES
FOR
COLLEGE
STUDENTS
AND
RECENT
GRADUATES

CAREER CENTER

CAREER CENTER

CAREER CENTER

CAREER CENTER

CAREER CENTER

CAREER CENTER

Professional Resumes Series

RESUMES
FOR
COLLEGE
STUDENTS
AND
RECENT
GRADUATES

The Editors of
VGM Career Horizons

Second Edition

VGM Career Horizons
NTC/Contemporary Publishing Company

Library of Congress Cataloging-in-Publication Data

Resumes for college students and recent graduates / the editors of
    VGM Career Horizons. — 2nd ed.
        p.   cm. — (VGM professional resumes series)
    ISBN 0-8442-4418-X
    1. Résumés (Employment)   2. College graduates—Employment.
3. College students—Employment.   I. VGM Career Horizons (Firm)
II. Series.
HF5383.R434   1998
650.14—dc21   97-50250
                                                        CIP

Acknowledgment
We would like to acknowledge the assistance of Kathy Siebel
in compiling and editing this book.

Published by VGM Career Horizons
A division of NTC/Contemporary Publishing Group, Inc.
4255 West Touhy Avenue, Lincolnwood (Chicago), Illinois 60712-1975 U.S.A.
International Standard Book Number: 0-8442-4418-X

4 5 6 7 8 9 0 VLP VLP 0 5 4 3 2 1

CONTENTS

Introduction

Your resume is your first impression on a prospective employer. Though you may be articulate, intelligent, and charming in person, a poor resume may prevent you from ever having the opportunity to demonstrate your interpersonal skills, because a poor resume may prevent you from ever being called for an interview. While few people have ever been hired solely on the basis of their resume, a well-written, well-organized resume can go a long way toward helping you land an interview. Your resume's main purpose is to get you that interview. The rest is up to you and the employer. If you both feel that you are right for the job and the job is right for you, chances are you will be hired.

A resume must catch the reader's attention yet still be easy to read and to the point. Resume styles have changed over the years. Today, brief and focused resumes are preferred. No longer do employers have the patience, or the time, to review several pages of solid type. A resume should be only one page long, if possible, and never more than two pages. Time is a precious commodity in today's business world and the resume that is concise and straightforward will usually be the one that gets noticed

Let's not make the mistake, though, of assuming that writing a brief resume means that you can take less care in preparing it. A successful resume takes time and thought, and if you are willing to make the effort, the rewards are well worth it. Think of your resume as a sales tool with the product being you. You want to sell yourself to a prospective employer. This book is designed to help you prepare a resume that will help you further your career—to land that next job, or first job, or to return to the work force after years of absence. So, read on. Make the effort and reap the rewards that a strong resume can being to your career. Let's get to it!

Chapter One

THE ELEMENTS OF A GOOD RESUME

A winning resume is made of the elements that employers are most interested in seeing when reviewing a job applicant. These basic elements are the essential ingredients of a successful resume and become the actual sections of your resume. The following is a list of elements that may be used in a resume. Some are essential; some are optional. We will be discussing these in this chapter in order to give you a better understanding of each element's role in the makeup of your resume:

1. Heading
2. Objective
3. Work Experience
4. Education
5. Honors
6. Activities
7. Certificates and Licenses
8. Professional Memberships
9. Special Skills
10. Personal Information
11. References

The first step in preparing your resume is to gather together information about yourself and your past accomplishments. Later you will refine this information, rewrite it in the most effective language, and organize it into the most attractive layout. First, let's take a look at each of these important elements individually.

Heading

The heading may seem to be a simple enough element in your resume, but be careful not to take it lightly. The heading should be placed at the top of your resume and should include your name, home address, and telephone numbers. If you can take calls at your current place of business, include your business number, since most employers will attempt to contact you during the business day. If this is not possible, or if you can afford it, purchase an answering machine that allows you to retrieve your messages while you are away from home. This way you can make sure you don't miss important phone calls. Always include your phone number on your resume. It is crucial that when prospective employers need to have immediate contact with you, they can.

Objective

When seeking a particular career path, it is important to list a job objective on your resume. This statement helps employers know the direction that you see yourself heading, so that they can determine whether your goals are in line with the position available. The objective is normally one sentence long and describes your employment goals clearly and concisely. See the sample resumes in this book for examples of objective statements.

The job objective will vary depending on the type of person you are, the field you are in, and the type of goals you have. It can be either specific or general, but it should always be to the point.

In some cases, this element is not necessary, but usually it is a good idea to include your objective. It gives your possible future employer an idea of where you are coming from and where you want to go.

The objective statement is better left out, however, if you are uncertain of the exact title of the job you seek. In such a case, the inclusion of an overly specific objective statement could result in your not being considered for a variety of acceptable positions; you should be sure to incorporate this information in your cover letter, instead.

Work Experience

This element is arguably the most important of them all. It will provide the central focus of your resume, so it is necessary that this section be as complete as possible. Only by examining your work experience in depth can you get to the heart of your accomplishments and present them in a way that demonstrates the strength of your qualifications. Of course, someone just out of school will have less work experience than someone who has been working for a number of years, but the amount of information isn't the most important thing—rather, how it is presented and how it highlights you as a person and as a worker will be what counts.

As you work on this section of your resume, be aware of the need for accuracy. You'll want to include all necessary information about each of your jobs, including job title, dates, employer, city, state, responsibilities, special projects, and accomplishments. Be sure to only list company accomplishments for which you were directly responsible. If you haven't participated in any special projects, that's all right—this area may not be relevant to certain jobs.

The most common way to list your work experience is in *reverse chronological order*. In other words, start with your most recent job and work your way backwards. This way your prospective employer sees your current (and often most important) job before seeing your past jobs. Your most recent position, if the most important, should also be the one that includes the most information, as compared to your previous positions. If you are just out of school, show your summer employment and part-time work, though in this case your education will most likely be more important than your work experience.

The following worksheets will help you gather information about your past jobs.

WORK EXPERIENCE
Job One:

Job Title _____

Dates _____

Employer _____

City, State _____

Major Duties _____

_____

_____

_____

_____

_____

_____

Special Projects _____

_____

_____

_____

Accomplishments _____

_____

_____

_____

_____

_____

_____

_____

Job Two:

Job Title _____

Dates _____

Employer _____

City, State _____

Major Duties _____

_____

_____

_____

_____

_____

_____

_____

Special Projects _____

_____

_____

_____

Accomplishments _____

_____

_____

_____

_____

_____

_____

_____

Job Three:

Job Title _____

Dates _____

Employer _____

City, State _____

Major Duties _____

_____

_____

_____

_____

_____

_____

Special Projects _____

_____

_____

_____

Accomplishments_____

_____

_____

_____

_____

_____

_____

_____

Job Four:

Job Title _____

Dates _____

Employer _____

City, State _____

Major Duties _____

_____

_____

_____

_____

_____

_____

Special Projects _____

_____

_____

_____

Accomplishments _____

_____

_____

_____

_____

_____

_____

_____

Education

Education is the second most important element of a resume. Your educational background is often a deciding factor in an employer's decision to hire you. Be sure to stress your accomplishments in school with the same finesse that you stressed your accomplishments at work. If you are looking for your first job, your education will be your greatest asset, since your work experience will most likely be minimal. In this case, the education section becomes the most important. You will want to be sure to include any degrees or certificates you received, your major area of concentration, any honors, and any relevant activities. Again, be sure to list your most recent schooling first. If you have completed graduate-level work, begin with that and work in reverse chronological order through your undergraduate education. If you have completed an undergraduate degree, you may choose whether to list your high school experience or not. This should be done only if your high school grade-point average was well above average.

The following worksheets will help you gather information for this section of your resume. Also included are supplemental worksheets for honors and for activities. Sometimes honors and activities are listed in a section separate from education, most often near the end of the resume.

EDUCATION

School _____

Major or Area of Concentration _____

Degree _____

Date _____

School _____

Major or Area of Concentration _____

Degree _____

Date _____

Honors

Here, you should list any awards, honors, or memberships in honorary societies that you have received. Usually these are of an academic nature, but they can also be for special achievement in sports, clubs, or other school activities. Always be sure to include the name of the organization honoring you and the date(s) received. Use the worksheet below to help gather your honors information.

HONORS

Honor: _____

Awarding Organization: _____

Date(s): _____

Honor: _____

Awarding Organization: _____

Date(s): _____

Honor: _____

Awarding Organization: _____

Date(s): _____

Honor: _____

Awarding Organization: _____

Date(s): _____

Activities

You may have been active in different organizations or clubs during your years at school; often an employer will look at such involvement as evidence of initiative and dedication. Your ability to take an active role, and even a leadership role, in a group should be included on your resume. Use the worksheet provided to list your activities and accomplishments in this area. In general, you should exclude any organization the name of which indicates the race, creed, sex, age, marital status, color, or nation of origin of its members.

ACTIVITIES

Organization/Activity: _____

Accomplishments: _____

_____

_____

Organization/Activity: _____

Accomplishments: _____

_____

_____

Organization/Activity: _____

Accomplishments: _____

_____

_____

Organization/Activity: _____

Accomplishments: _____

_____

_____

As your work experience increases through the years, your school activities and honors will play less of a role in your resume, and eventually you will most likely only list your degree and any major honors you received. This is due to the fact that, as time goes by, your job performance becomes the most important element in your resume. Through time, your resume should change to reflect this.

Certificates and Licenses

The next potential element of your resume is certificates and licenses. You should list these if the job you are seeking requires them and you, of course, have acquired them. If you have applied for a license, but have not yet received it, use the phrase "application pending."

License requirements vary by state. If you have moved or you are planning to move to another state, be sure to check with the appropriate board or licensing agency in the state in which you are applying for work to be sure that you are aware of all licensing requirements.

Always be sure that all of the information you list is completely accurate. Locate copies of your licenses and certificates and check the exact date and name of the accrediting agency. Use the following worksheet to list your licenses and certificates.

CERTIFICATES AND LICENSES

Name of License: _____

Licensing Agency: _____

Date Issued: _____

Name of License: _____

Licensing Agency: _____

Date Issued: _____

Name of License: _____

Licensing Agency: _____

Date Issued: _____

Professional Memberships

Another potential element in your resume is a section listing professional memberships. Use this section to list involvement in professional associations, unions, and similar organizations. It is to your advantage to list any professional memberships that pertain to the job you are seeking. Be sure to include the dates of your involvement and whether you took part in any special activities or held any offices within the organization. Use the following worksheet to gather your information.

PROFESSIONAL MEMBERSHIPS

Name of Organization: _____

Offices Held: _____

Activities: _____

Date(s): _____

Name of Organization: _____

Offices Held: _____

Activities: _____

Date(s): _____

Name of Organization: _____

Offices Held: _____

Activities: _____

Date(s): _____

Name of Organization: _____

Offices Held: _____

Activities: _____

Date(s): _____

Special Skills

This section of your resume is set aside for mentioning any special abilities you have that could relate to the job you are seeking. This is the part of your resume where you have the opportunity to demonstrate certain talents and experiences that are not necessarily a part of your educational or work experience. Common examples include fluency in a foreign language, or knowledge of a particular computer application.

Special skills can encompass a wide range of your talents—remember to be sure that whatever skills you list relate to the type of work you are looking for.

Personal Information

Some people include "Personal" information on their resumes. This is not generally recommended, but you might wish to include it if you think that something in your personal life, such as a hobby or talent, has some bearing on the position you are seeking. This type of information is often referred to at the beginning of an interview, when it is used as an "ice breaker." Of course, personal information regarding age, marital status, race, religion, or sexual preference should never appear on any resume.

References

References are not usually listed on the resume, but a prospective employer needs to know that you have references who may be contacted if necessary. All that is necessary to include in your resume regarding references is a sentence at the bottom stating, "References are available upon request." If a prospective employer requests a list of references, be sure to have one ready. Also, check with whomever you list to see if it is all right for you to use them as a reference. Forewarn them that they may receive a call regarding a reference for you. This way they can be prepared to give you the best reference possible.

Chapter Two

WRITING YOUR RESUME

Now that you have gathered together all of the information for each of the sections of your resume, it's time to write out each section in a way that will get the attention of whoever is reviewing it. The type of language you use in your resume will affect its success. You want to take the information you have gathered and translate it into a language that will cause a potential employer to sit up and take notice.

Resume writing is not like expository writing or creative writing. It embodies a functional, direct writing style and focuses on the use of action words. By using action words in your writing, you more effectively stress past accomplishments. Action words help demonstrate your initiative and highlight your talents. Always use verbs that show strength and reflect the qualities of a "doer." By using action words, you characterize yourself as a person who takes action, and this will impress potential employers.

The following is a list of verbs commonly used in resume writing. Use this list to choose the action words that can help your resume become a strong one:

administered

advised

analyzed

arranged

assembled

assumed responsibility

billed

built

carried out

channeled

collected

communicated

compiled

completed

conducted

contacted

contracted

coordinated

counseled

created

cut

designed

determined

developed

directed

dispatched

distributed

documented

edited

established

expanded

functioned as

gathered

handled

hired

implemented

improved

inspected

interviewed

introduced

invented

maintained

managed

met with

motivated

negotiated

operated

orchestrated

ordered

organized

oversaw

performed

planned

prepared

presented

produced

programmed

published

purchased

recommended

recorded

reduced

referred

represented

researched

reviewed

saved

screened

served as

served on

sold

suggested

supervised

taught

tested

trained

typed

wrote

Now take a look at the information you put down on the work experience worksheets. Take that information and rewrite it in paragraph form, using verbs to highlight your actions and accomplishments. Let's look at an example, remembering that what matters here is the writing style, and not the particular job responsibilities given in our sample.

WORK EXPERIENCE
Regional Sales Manager

Manager of sales representatives from seven states. Responsible for twelve food chain accounts in the East. In charge of directing the sales force in planned selling toward specific goals. Supervisor and trainer of new sales representatives. Consulting for customers in the areas of inventory management and quality control.

Special Projects: Coordinator and sponsor of annual food industry sales seminar.

Accomplishments: Monthly regional volume went up 25 percent during my tenure while, at the same time, a proper sales/cost ratio was maintained. Customer/company relations improved significantly.

Below is the rewritten version of this information, using action words. Notice how much stronger it sounds.

WORK EXPERIENCE
Regional Sales Manager

Managed sales representatives from seven states. Handled twelve food chain accounts in the eastern United States. Directed the sales force in planned selling towards specific goals. Supervised and trained new sales representatives. Consulted for customers in the areas of inventory management and quality control. Coordinated and sponsored the annual Food Industry Seminar. Increased monthly regional volume 25 percent and helped to improve customer/company relations during my tenure.

Another way of constructing the work experience section is by using actual job descriptions. Job descriptions are rarely written using the proper resume language, but they do include all the information necessary to create this section of your resume. Take the description of one of the jobs your are including on your resume (if you have access to it), and turn it into an action-oriented paragraph. Below is an example of a job description followed by a version of the same description written using action words. Again, pay attention to the style of writing, as the details of your own work experience will be unique.

PUBLIC ADMINISTRATOR I

Responsibilities: Coordinate and direct public services to meet the needs of the nation, state, or community. Analyze problems; work with special committees and public agencies; recommend solutions to governing bodies.

Aptitudes and Skills: Ability to relate to and communicate with people; solve complex problems through analysis; plan, organize, and implement policies and programs. Knowledge of political systems; financial management; personnel administration; program evaluation; organizational theory.

WORK EXPERIENCE
Public Administrator I

Wrote pamphlets and conducted discussion groups to inform citizens of legislative processes and consumer issues. Organized and supervised 25 interviewers. Trained interviewers in effective communication skills.

Now that you have learned how to word your resume, you are ready for the next step in your quest for a winning resume: assembly and layout.

Chapter Three

ASSEMBLY AND LAYOUT

*A*t this point, you've gathered all the necessary information for your resume, and you've rewritten it using the language necessary to impress potential employers. Your next step is to assemble these elements in a logical order and then to lay them out on the page neatly and attractively in order to achieve the desired effect: getting that interview.

Assembly

The order of the elements in a resume makes a difference in its overall effect. Obviously, you would not want to put your name and address in the middle of the resume or your special skills section at the top. You want to put the elements in an order that stresses your most important achievements, not the less pertinent information. For example, if you recently graduated from school and have no full-time work experience, you will want to list your education before you list any part-time jobs you may have held during school. On the other hand, if you have been gainfully employed for several years and currently hold an important position in your company, you will want to list your work experience ahead of your education, which has become less pertinent with time.

There are some elements that are always included in your resume and some that are optional. Following is a list of essential and optional elements:

Essential	*Optional*
Name	Job Objective
Address	Honors
Phone Number	Special Skills
Work Experience	Professional Memberships
Education	Activities
References Phrase	Certificates and Licenses
	Personal Information

Your choice of optional sections depends on your own background and employment needs. Always use information that will put you and your abilities in a favorable light. If your honors are impressive, then be sure to include them in your resume. If your activities in school demonstrate particular talents necessary for the job you are seeking, then allow space for a section on activities. Each resume is unique, just as each person is unique.

Types of Resumes

So far, our discussion about resumes has involved the most common type—the *reverse chronological* resume, in which your most recent job is listed first and so on. This is the type of resume usually preferred by human resources directors, and it is the one most frequently used. However, in some cases this style of presentation is not the most effective way to highlight your skills and accomplishments.

For someone reentering the work force after many years or someone looking to change career fields, the *functional resume* may work best. This type of resume focuses more on achievement and less on the sequence of your work history. In the functional resume, your experience is presented by what you have accomplished and the skills you have developed in your past work.

A functional resume can be assembled from the same information you collected for your chronological resume. The main difference lies in how you organize this information. Essentially, the work experience section becomes two sections, with your job duties and accomplishments comprising one section and your employer's name, city, state, your position, and the dates employed making up another section. The first section is placed near the top of the resume, just below the job objective section, and can be called *Accomplishments* or *Achievements*. The second section, containing the bare essentials of your employment history, should come after the accomplishments section and can be titled *Work Experience* or *Employment History*. The other sections of your resume remain the same. The work experience section is the only one affected in the functional resume. By placing the section that focuses on your achievements first, you thereby draw attention to these achievements. This puts less emphasis on who you worked for and more emphasis on what you did and what you are capable of doing.

For someone changing careers, emphasis on skills and achievements is essential. The identities of previous employers, which may be unrelated to one's new job field, need to be down-played. The functional resume accomplishes this task. For some-one reentering the work force after many years, a functional resume is the obvious choice. If you lack full-time work experi-ence, you will need to draw attention away from this fact and in-stead focus on your skills and abilities gained possibly through volunteer activities or part-time work. Education may also play a more important role in this resume.

Which type of resume is right for you will depend on your own personal circumstances. It may be helpful to create a chrono-logical *and* a functional resume and then compare the two to find out which is more suitable. The sample resumes found in this book include both chronological and functional resumes. Use these resumes as guides to help you decide on the content and appearance of your own resume.

Layout

Once you have decided which elements to include in your resume and you have arranged them in an order that makes sense and emphasizes your achievements and abilities, then it is time to work on the physical layout of your resume.

There is no single appropriate layout that applies to every re-sume, but there are a few basic rules to follow in putting your re-sume on paper:

1. Leave a comfortable margin on the sides, top, and bot-tom of the page (usually 1 to 1½ inches).

2. Use appropriate spacing between the sections (usually 2 to 3 line spaces are adequate).

3. Be consistent in the *type* of headings you use for the dif-ferent sections of your resume. For example, if you capi-talize the heading EMPLOYMENT HISTORY, don't use initial capitals and underlining for a heading of equal importance, such as Education.

4. Always try to fit your resume onto one page. If you are having trouble fitting all your information onto one page, perhaps you are trying to say too much. Try to edit out any repetitive or unnecessary information or possibly shorten descriptions of earlier jobs. Be ruthless. Maybe you've included too many optional sections.

CHRONOLOGICAL RESUME

JUAN C. GARCIA

2103 AFTON STREET

TEMPLE HILL, MARYLAND 20748

HOME (301) 555-2419

EDUCATION:

Columbia University, New York, NY
Majors: Business, Philosophy
Degree expected: Bachelor of Arts, 1998
Grade point average; 3.5
Regents Scholarship recipient
Columbia University Scholarship recipient

EXPERIENCE:
7/97-9/97

Graduate Business Library, Columbia University, NY
General library duties. Entered new students and books onto computer files.
Gave out microfiche. Reserved and distributed materials.

9/96-5/97

German Department, Columbia University, NY
Performed general office duties. Offered extensive information assistance by phone
and in person. Collated and proofread class materials. Assisted professors in the
gathering of class materials.

6/96-9/96

Loan Collections Department, Columbia University, NY
Initiated new filing system for the office. Checked arrears in Bursar's Office during
registration period.

9/95-5/96

School of Continuing Education, Columbia University, NY
Involved in heavy public contact as well as general clerical duties.

SPECIAL ABILITIES:

Fluent in Spanish. Currently studying German. Can program in BASIC.
Excellent research skills.

REFERENCES:

Available on request

FUNCTIONAL RESUME

REVA POPERMAN
Gerber Hall
100 Westwood Ave.
Los Angeles, CA 90289
213/555-1562

CAREER OBJECTIVE

A career in the field of Human Resources.

EDUCATION

UCLA, Los Angeles, CA
Bachelor of Arts in Business
Expected June 1998

HONORS

Phi Beta Kappa
Dean's List five semesters

ACTIVITIES

President, Student Government
Resident Advisor
Homecoming Planning Committee
Volleyball Team

WORK EXPERIENCE

TPT, Inc., Burbank, CA
Human Resources Intern, 8/97 to Present

Assist Human Resources Director in areas of personnel acquisition and evaluation. Receive
and file resumes. Administer tests to prospective employees. Set up appointments for interviews.

UCLA, Los Angeles, CA
Research/Office Assistant, 9/96 to 6/97

Researched and compiled materials for department professors. Arranged filing system and
supervisor's library. Organized department inventory.

REFERENCES AVAILABLE

Don't let the idea of having to tell every detail about your life get in the way of producing a resume that is simple and straightforward. The more compact your resume, the easier it will be to read and the better an impression it will make for you.

In some cases, the resume will not fit on a single page, even after extensive editing. In such cases, the resume should be printed on two pages so as not to compromise clarity or appearance. Each page of a two-page resume should be marked clearly with your name and the page number, e.g., "Judith Ramirez, page 1 of 2." The pages should then be stapled together.

Try experimenting with various layouts until you find one that looks good to you. Always show your final layout to other people and ask them what they like or dislike about it, and what impresses them most about your resume. Make sure that is what you want most to emphasize. If it isn't, you may want to consider making changes in your layout until the necessary information is emphasized. Use the sample resumes in this book to get some ideas for laying out your resume.

Putting Your Resume in Print

Your resume should be typed or printed on good quality 8½" × 11" bond paper. You want to make as good an impression as possible with your resume; therefore, quality paper is a necessity. If you have access to a word processor with a good printer, or know of someone who does, make use of it. Typewritten resumes should only be used when there are no other options available.

After you have produced a clean original, you will want to make duplicate copies of it. Usually a copy shop is your best bet for producing copies without smudges or streaks. Make sure you have the copy shop use quality bond paper for all copies of your resume. Ask for a sample copy before they run your entire order. After copies are made, check each copy for cleanliness and clarity.

Another more costly option is to have your resume typeset and printed by a printer. This will provide the most attractive resume of all. If you anticipate needing a lot of copies of your resume, the cost of having it typeset may be justified.

Proofreading

After you have finished typing the master copy of your resume and before you go to have it copied or printed, you must thoroughly check it for typing and spelling errors. Have several people read it over just in case you may have missed an error. Misspelled words and typing mistakes will not make a good impression on a prospective employer, as they are a bad reflection on your writing ability and your attention to detail. With thorough and conscientious proofreading, these mistakes can be avoided.

The following are some rules of capitalization and punctuation that may come in handy when proofreading your resume:

Rules of Capitalization

- Capitalize proper nouns, such as names of schools, colleges, and universities, names of companies, and brand names of products.

- Capitalize major words in the names and titles of books, tests, and articles that appear in the body of your resume.

- Capitalize words in major section headings of your resume.

- Do not capitalize words just because they seem important.

- When in doubt, consult a manual of style such as *Words Into Type* (Prentice-Hall), or *The Chicago Manual of Style* (The University of Chicago Press). Your local library can help you locate these and other reference books.

Rules of Punctuation

- Use a comma to separate words in a series.

- Use a semicolon to separate series of words that already include commas within the series.

- Use a semicolon to separate independent clauses that are not joined by a conjunction.

- Use a period to end a sentence.

- Use a colon to show that the examples or details that follow expand or amplify the preceding phrase.

- Avoid the use of dashes.

- Avoid the use of brackets.

- If you use any punctuation in an unusual way in your resume, be consistent in its use.

- Whenever you are uncertain, consult a style manual.

Chapter Four

THE COVER LETTER

*O*nce your resume has been assembled, laid out, and printed to your satisfaction, the next and final step before distribution is to write your cover letter. Though there may be instances where you deliver your resume in person, most often you will be sending it through the mail. Resumes sent through the mail always need an accompanying letter that briefly introduces you and your resume. The purpose of the cover letter is to get a potential employer to read your resume, just as the purpose of your resume is to get that same potential employer to call you for an interview.

Like your resume, your cover letter should be clean, neat, and direct. A cover letter usually includes the following information:

1. Your name and address (unless it already appears on your personal letterhead).

2. The date.

3. The name and address of the person and company to whom you are sending your resume.

4. The salutation ("Dear Mr." or "Dear Ms." followed by the person's last name, or "To Whom It May Concern" if you are answering a blind ad).

5. An opening paragraph explaining why you are writing (in response to an ad, the result of a previous meeting, at the suggestion of someone you both know) and indicating that you are interested in whatever job is being offered.

6. One or two more paragraphs that tell why you want to work for the company and what qualifications and experience you can bring to that company.

7. A final paragraph that closes the letter and requests that you be contacted for an interview. You may mention here that your references are available upon request.

8. The closing ("Sincerely," or "Yours Truly," followed by your signature with your name typed under it).

Your cover letter, including all of the information above, should be no more than one page in length. The language used should be polite, businesslike, and to the point. Do not attempt to tell your life story in the cover letter. A long and cluttered letter will only serve to put off the reader. Remember, you only need to mention a few of your accomplishments and skills in the cover letter. The rest of your information is in your resume. Each and every achievement should not be mentioned twice. If your cover letter is a success, your resume will be read and all pertinent information reviewed by your prospective employer.

Producing the Cover Letter

Cover letters should always be typed individually, since they are always written to particular individuals and companies. Never use a form letter for your cover letter. Cover letters cannot be copied or reproduced like resumes. Each one should be as personal as possible. Of course, once you have written and rewritten your first cover letter to the point where you are satisfied with it, you certainly can use similar wording in subsequent letters.

After you have typed your cover letter on quality bond paper, be sure to proofread it as thoroughly as you did your resume. Again, spelling errors are a sure sign of carelessness, and you don't want that to be a part of your first impression on a prospective employer. Make sure to handle the letter and resume carefully to avoid any smudges, and then mail both your cover letter and resume in an appropriate sized envelope. Be sure to keep an accurate record of all the resumes you send out and the results of each mailing, either in a separate notebook or on individual 3 × 5" index cards.

Numerous sample cover letters appear at the end of the book. Use them as models for your own cover letter or to get an idea of how cover letters are put together. Remember, every one is unique and depends on the particular circumstances of the individual writing it and the job for which he or she is applying.

Now the job of writing your resume and cover letter is complete. About a week after mailing resumes and cover letters to potential employers, you will want to contact them by telephone. Confirm that your resume arrived, and ask whether an interview might be possible. Getting your foot in the door during this call is half the battle of a job search, and a strong resume and cover letter will help you immeasurably.

Chapter Five

SAMPLE RESUMES

This chapter contains dozens of sample resumes for people pursuing a wide variety of jobs and careers.

There are many different styles of resumes in terms of graphic layout and presentation of information. These samples also represent people with varying amounts of education and experience. Use these samples to model your own resume after. Choose one resume, or borrow elements from several different rcsumes to help you construct your own.

EUNICE T. BODEANE
1221 E. Cambridge Avenue
Lynn, MA 02129

617/555-8800

OBJECTIVE: A position as publicist with an arts organization.

WORK HISTORY: **Boston Opera Company, Boston, MA**
P.R. Assistant, 1996-Present
Compose press releases and public service announcements
that publicize opera events. Develop contacts with Boston
entertainment columnists that result in extensive coverage.
Maintain calendar of advertising deadlines. Write ad copy
for print and radio.

Sandra Watt Agency, Boston, MA
Editorial/P.R. Assistant, 1995-1996
Edited technical and literary manuscripts. Compiled a directory
of Boston editors and publishers for agency use. Organized an
educational workshop for local writers.

EDUCATION: **Ithaca University, Ithaca, New York**
B.S. in Advertising, June 1996

Courses: Marketing Techniques, Advertising, Corporate Public
Relations, P.R. techniques.

HONORS: Sigma Kappa Nu Honorary Society
Honors in Advertising
Dean's List
Myron T. Kapp Public Relations Award

ACTIVITIES: Student Government Representative
Homecoming Committee
Soccer Club

REFERENCES: Provided on request.

ALLISON SPRINGS
15 Hilton House
Colorado Women's College
Denver, CO 80220
303/555-2550

Job Sought: Position within a government or nonprofit agency that can benefit from
my organizational and marketing skills.

Skills and Experience:

Negotiating Skills: Developed negotiating skills through participation in student government
which enabled me to persuade others of the advantages of compromise.

Promotional Skills: Contributed greatly to my successful campaign for class office
(Junior Class Vice President) through the effective use of posters, displays,
and other visual aids. Participated in committee projects and fund-raising efforts
that netted $15,000 for the junior class project.

People Skills: As Junior Class Vice President, balanced the concerns of different groups
in order to reach a common goal. As a claims interviewer with a state public
assistance agency, dealt with people under stressful circumstances. As a research
assistant with a law firm, interacted with both lawyers and clerical workers.
As a lifeguard, learned how to manage groups.

Education: Colorado Women's College
Bachelor of Arts in Political Science
Degree expected June 1998
Vice President Junior Class
Student Council
Harvest Committee

Work Experience: McCall, McCrow & McCoy, Westrow, CO
Research Assistant, January 1996 to present

Department of Public Assistance, Denver, CO
Claims Interviewer, September 1995 - December 1995

Shilo Pool, Shilo, NE
Lifeguard, 1991 - 1994

References: Provided on request

RUTH M. DAVID
572 First Street
Brooklyn, NY 11215
(212) 555-4328

Education	Princeton University, Princeton, NJ
Degree Expected: M.S. in Communications, June 1998
Class Rank: Top ten percent
Editor of Communications Journal

University of Wisconsin, Madison, WI
B.A. in Political Science, May 1996
Dean's List
Marching Band Section Leader |
| Work History | Boston Theatre Co., Boston, MA
P.R. Internship, 6/97 to 9/97
Composed press releases and public service announcements which publicized theatre events. Oversaw production of posters, flyers, and programs. Sold subscriptions and advertising space. |
| Other Experience | Citizens Action Group, New York, NY
Field Manager, 6/96 to 9/96
Promoted public awareness of state legislative process and issues of toxic waste, utility control, and consumer legislation. Demonstrated effective fundraising skills.

University of Wisconsin, Madison, WI
Resident Assistant, Office of Residential Life, 9/95 to 6/96
Administered all aspects of student affairs in university residence halls, including program planning, discipline, and individual group counseling. Directed achievement of student goals through guidance of the residence hall council. Implemented all university policies. |

Page 1 of 2

Other Experience (cont.)

        University of Wisconsin, Madison, WI
        Staff Training Lecturer, 8/95 to 12/95
        Conducted workshops for residence hall staff on counseling,
        effective communication, and conflict resolution.

Special Skills   Knowledge of WordPerfect 6.1 and Lotus 1-2-3
        Knowledge of Spanish and French
        CPR certified

References   Available on Request.

TERRI BAKKEMO

700 Thornborough Rd.
Chattanooga, TN 75221
615/555-2111

CAREER OBJECTIVE

A career in the field of broadcast journalism where I can utilize my experience in writing, editing and research.

EDUCATION

HOWARD UNIVERSITY, Washington, DC
Bachelor of Arts, Journalism, expected June 1998

WORK EXPERIENCE

WDC-TV, Washington, DC
Research Assistant/News Department, Summer 1997
Assisted in the production of a news show. Served as a copy aide. Worked at UPI office during congressional hearings. Handled general research duties.

CAPITOL MAGAZINE, Washington, DC
Editorial Assistant to Senior Editor, Summer 1996
Coordinated an organized system of manuscript flow between editors. Assisted in editing and proofreading copy. Rewrote news articles and planned new stories and layout ideas.

CHATTANOOGA NEWS, Chattanooga, TN
Intern, Summer 1995
Assisted in layout, editing and reporting for local newspaper. Wrote and edited articles.

PARK ADVERTISING, INC., Chattanooga, TN
Creative Department Intern, Summer 1994
Handled proofreading and editing of copy. Assisted in demographic research.

HONORS

Harris Academic Scholarship, 1996, 1997
Dean's List

REFERENCES

Available on request

EDUARDO LOPEZ
6 E. Columbus Drive
College Park, MD 20740
410-555-3938

Goal: Research technician position that allows me to use my training in physics.

Education: University of Maryland, College Park, MD
B.S., Physics, June 1997

Relevant Coursework

Plasma Physics
Medical Instrumentation
Statistics
Research Methodology

Honors

Dean's List
Sigma Pi Sigma, Physics Honor Society

Experience: University of Maryland, Physics Department
Research Associate
June 1997 to Present

Conduct literature research and create literature studies to support work of department. Record and analyze research data. Contribute to technical reports and publications.

Huntington Burroughs Pharmaceutical Inc.
Student Intern
Summer 1996

Assisted senior researcher with data input, statistical analysis, and computer model development.

References: Available on Request

YVONNE KORBIN
33 E. Lincoln
Chicago, IL 60655
Tel. (312) 555-2029
Fax (312) 555-4394

GOAL: A marketing/publicity position in the recording industry

WORK HISTORY: PTO PRODUCTION, Evanston IL
                    Public Relations/Marketing Assistant
                    Dates: 5/97 to Present

                    Duties: Assist P.R. Director with all duties, including radio promotion
                    and retail marketing. Coordinate radio and print interviews for artists.
                    Manage all details of office including scheduling, record keeping, and
                    document preparation.

                    WCHO RADIO, Chicago, IL
                    Music Director
                    Dates: 6/96 to 5/97

                    Duties: Selected appropriate music for a contemporary jazz format.
                    Oversaw daily operations of music library and programming
                    department. Supervised a staff of six.

EDUCATION: Northwestern Illinois University, Evanston, IL
                    B.A. in Arts Management, May 1997

                    G.P.A. in major: 3.8

                    Received Ross Hunter Arts Management Scholarship

SKILLS: Fluent in French
                    Working knowledge of WordPerfect 6.0 and Lotus 1-2-3

References on Request

ANDREW ROBERTS
998 Essex Blvd. #32
Toledo, OH 43601
419/555-4098

OBJECTIVE:	A position in the field of finance.
EDUCATION:	**WESTERN UNIVERSITY,** Toledo, OH Graduate School of Business Administration M.B.A. expected, June 1998 Concentration: Finance Finance Club Student Advisory Board
	UNIVERSITY OF ILLINOIS, Chicago, IL B.A. in Economics, June 1996 Summa Cum Laude Phi Beta Kappa Student Government Vice President
WORK EXPERIENCE:	**Household Finance Co.,** Toledo, OH Financial Accounting Intern, 9/97 to Present Review and process loan applications, including establishing collateral, checking credit ratings, verifying employment status. Discuss loan terms with new customers, and handle all related paperwork.
	Bank of Ohio, Toledo, OH Commercial Loan Intern, Summer 1996 Provided financial data to commercial account officers. Handled past-due receivables.
	University of Illinois, Chicago, IL Assistant, Accounts Payable Department, 1995 to 1996 Assisted with data input, preparation of check requests, and disbursements. Tracked accounts receivable and accounts payable.
REFERENCES:	Available upon request

BERLINDA S. BROWNE

66 OVERLAND AVE. * TOLEDO, OH 43601 * 419/555-3600

CAREER GOAL: Medical Assistant

EDUCATION: Anderson Community College, Toledo, OH
Medical Assistant Program Certificate,
expected December 1997

EXPERIENCE: Toledo Hospital, Toledo, OH
Internship, 1/97-5/97

--Prepared patients for examination and x-rays.

--Handled routine lab procedures.

--Interviewed and scheduled patients.

--Assisted with medical examinations and minor surgery.

--Sterilized instruments.

--Organized medical records.

MEMBERSHIPS: American Association of Medical Assistants

REFERENCES: Submitted upon request

SAMUEL TRAVIS SHAVERS

15 E. Greenview St. #333
Richmond, VA 18978
804/555-3903

EDUCATION

<u>University of Virginia</u>, Richmond, VA
B.A. in Journalism, expected June 1998

Hawkins Journalism Scholarship, 1996 and 1997
Intern with WRCH-TV
Vice President, Senior Class

WRITING EXPERIENCE

* Served as Senior Editor of campus newspaper; selected articles; approved editorials; edited and wrote
copy; supervised seven writers.

*Assisted in the editing of literary magazine <u>Flight</u>; proofread and edited copy.

*Researched stories for local television station.

*Wrote a weekly column for campus newspaper; actively pursued investigative reporting; handled events both
on campus and in the local community.

*Created design and layout for 1997 Freshman Handbook; assisted with typesetting and offset printing of handbook.

WORK HISTORY

University of Virginia, Richmond, VA
Senior Editor, Campus Newspaper, 1997 to Present

Editor, <u>Flight</u>, 1997

Designer, Freshman Handbook, 1997

Writer, Campus Newspaper, 1996-1997

WRCH-TV, Richmond, VA
Intern, 1996

MEMBERSHIPS

Association of College Journalists
Virginia Literary Society

REFERENCES

Available upon request

MARGARET WEIDLIN

333 Market St. #608
San Francisco, CA 98911
415/555-3526

Job Sought:	Women's Fashion Designer
Education:	PARKWOOD COLLEGE OF DESIGN, San Francisco, CA M.A. in Fashion Design, June 1997 NORTHWESTERN UNIVERSITY, Evanston, IL B.A. in Art History, 1992
Employer:	DAVIE WEAR, INC., San Francisco, CA Assistant Fashion Coordinator, 1995-Present
Skills and Accomplishments:	*Prepare clothing for display. *Evaluate and select fabrics. *Design patterns for fabric. *Coordinate window displays.
References:	Susan DeGeorge, Owner Davie Wear, Inc. 415/555-5958, ext. 332 Alex Rosenthal, Instructor Parkwood College of Design 415/555-4900, ext. 839 Design Portfolio Available Upon Request

THEODORE L. MCDONALD

2107 Adams St. #9
Austin, TX 78711
512/555-7665

JOB SOUGHT

Dietician/Nutritionist

EDUCATION

University of Texas, Austin, TX
B.S. in Nutrition, June 1997

HONORS

Speilberg Nutrition Award
Dean's List, four semesters

EMPLOYMENT HISTORY

University of Texas, Austin, TX
Assistant Nutritionist, September 1995-Present

Have planned over 250 menus with Head Nutritionist. Oversee interviewing and hiring of student workers.

Austin Hospital, Austin, TX
Assistant to Head Dietician, Summers 1995 and 1996

Assisted with menus and meal planning. Selected and delivered meals to special diet patients.

REFERENCES

Available upon request

SAGU RUGAT

888 S. Evers Street
Trenton, NJ 08778

——

Telephone 609/555-4903

GOAL: Assistant editor for book publisher

EDUCATION: University of Illinois
Bachelor of Arts Degree, June 1997

Major: English   G.P.A. in Major: 4.0

SKILLS: Familiar with University of Chicago Manual of Style
Excellent written and oral communication skills
Able to handle and prioritize multiple assignments
Excellent attention to detail
Computer literate, with knowledge of WordPerfect 6.0
    and PageMaker programs

EXPERIENCE: **Curtiss Publishing, Trenton, NJ**
Editorial Assistant, August 1997-Present

Assist editorial staff with all aspects of book production. Schedule
and track progress of projects. Proofread manuscripts. Type
book contracts and correspondence, read submissions.

University of Illinois Press, Champaign, IL
Student Intern

Provided general clerical support for university press. Did fact
checking and proofreading.

REFERENCES AVAILABLE

STANLEY TRUMBULL

3 S. Sioux Trail
Ottawa, Ontario, Canada K1P 5N2
613/555-1782

OBJECTIVE: A career in the field of anthropology

EDUCATION: UNIVERSITY OF OTTAWA, Ontario, Canada
B.A. in Anthropology, expected June 1998

HONORS: Dean's List, 1997
Phillips Anthropology Award, 1997

**EMPLOYMENT
HISTORY:** OTTAWA UNIVERSITY, Ontario, Canada
Department of Animal Behavior
Research Assistant, 9/97 - Present
Input data for animal behavior studies. Maintained lab equipment.
Monitored animals and recorded data.

OTTAWA UNIVERSITY, Ontario, Canada
Admissions Office
Student Assistant, 9/96 - 4/97
Conducted campus tours. Processed applications. Assisted in student
recruitment and general public relations.

PARKER & PARKER, Detroit, MI
Office Assistant, 6/96 - 9/96
Handled data entry, processing orders, phones.

ACTIVITIES: Anthropology Club, 1996-Present
Student Government Representative, Fall 1996

REFERENCES: Available upon request

REBECCA PORTER UPJOHN

100 West Tenth St.
Bloomington, IN 46703
317/555-3893

OBJECTIVE: A career in photography

EDUCATION

INDIANA STATE UNIVERSITY, Bloomington, IN
Bachelor of Arts, Visual Communications, June 1997
Emphasis in Photography

Coursework included:
Studio Lighting
Bank Lighting
Advertising/Product Photography
Photojournalism
Portrait Photography

WORK EXPERIENCE

FREELANCE PHOTOGRAPHER, June 1997 to Present
Handle advertising, publication, passport, and portrait photography.

INDIANA STATE UNIVERSITY, Bloomington, IN
PHOTOGRAPHER, MEDIA CENTER, 1996 - 1997
Worked directly with designer to fulfill the university's photographic needs. Used high-speed film to photograph dramatic events in existing light. Contributed photographs to university publications. Mastered standard film processing.

INDIANA STATE UNIVERSITY, Bloomington, IN
STUDENT ASSISTANT, BLOOMINGTON LIBRARY, 1995-1996
Assisted students in locating materials within the library and on-line. Worked check-out desk. Shelved and cataloged new materials.

Page 1 of 2

Rebecca Porter Upjohn
Page 2 of 2

EXHIBITS

Bloomington Library, 1996
Parker Gallery, 1996
Community Show, 1997
Campus Center, 1997

MEMBERSHIPS

Women in Photography
Designers in Progress
Communications Club
Advertising Club

PORTFOLIO AND REFERENCES AVAILABLE

Christine Harding
3333 N. Halen Ave. #3B
Toronto, Ontario, Canada M6P 4C7
416/555-2333

Education:

Toronto School of Law, Toronto, Ontario, Canada
Juris Doctor, expected June 1998
Area of Concentration: Health Care Litigation

University of California, Irvine, CA
B.S. in Biology, May 1995
Summa Cum Laude

Work Experience:

Tannen & Hope, Toronto, Ontario, Canada
Intern, 1/96 - Present
~Draft legal documents.
~Assist in the preparation of cases for trial.
~Conduct legal research.
~File motions with the court.

Skills:

Fluent in Spanish
Knowledge of Sign Language

Memberships:

Student Government Association
Progressive Law Coalition
Kappa Phi Honorary Society

References:

Provided on request

PETER PERKINS

60 Martin Drive
Milwaukee, WI 53201
414/555-1111

OBJECTIVE: A career in the manufacturing field

EDUCATION:

Milwaukee Institute of Technology, Milwaukee, WI
Bachelor of Science in Manufacturing Engineering Technology,
expected May 1998

Relevant Courses:

Machine Design	Planning
Manufacturing Analysis	Strength of Materials
Work Measurement	Motion Analysis
Control Systems	Quality Assurance
Technical Writing	Statics

EMPLOYMENT
HISTORY:

Wisconsin Manufacturing Co., Milwaukee, WI
 Forklift Driver, Summers 1996, 1997
 Drove forklifts. Repaired and serviced heavy machinery.

Penner Furniture, Inc., West Allis, WI
Warehouse Assistant, 1994-1996
Prepared furniture for delivery. Organized furniture stock.
Delivered furniture. Assisted in construction of furniture racks.

MEMBERSHIPS: Society of Manufacturing Engineers

REFERENCES: Submitted on request

BRIDGETT TERRY
4444 24th Street
Los Angeles, CA 91809
213/555-3411

OBJECTIVE

A position in personnel administration.

EDUCATION: PERSONNEL MANAGEMENT INSTITUTE
Lorminon College, Dallas, TX
Certificate of Completion
Summer 1997

UNIVERSITY OF CALIFORNIA AT BERKELEY
Bachelor's Degree in Economics, 1992

HONORS: Personnel Management Institute Dean's Award, 1997
UCSB Economics Scholarship, 1990-1991
Elected Student Government Secretary, 1991
Gamma Kappa Phi Honorary Society, 1991-1992

EXPERIENCE: WOODBINE & CO., Los Angeles, CA
Payroll Specialist, 1993 - Present

Determine job grading system. Evaluate jobs. Maintain employee budget. Conduct performance appraisals. Decide wage increases and adjustments. Set salary ranges. Write job descriptions. Coordinate compensation surveys. Gather data on vacations, sick time, and leaves of absence.

REFERENCES: Available on request.

KRISTINE HINCH
5222 38th St.
Washington, DC 20013
202/555-2003

Objective:	A career in Business Management
Education:	<u>Georgetown University</u>, Washington, DC M.B.A. expected June 1998 Area of Concentration: Financial Management/Accounting Management <u>Parker College</u>, Parker, IA B.A. June 1996 Major: Economics Minor: Political Science
Work Experience:	**Georgetown University, Washington, DC** **Analytical Studies Intern, 1997 - Present** Collecting and organizing data for a university finance study. Conducting library research. Will contribute to draft of final report. **Parker College, Parker, IA** **Resident Hall Assistant, 1994 - 1996** Oversaw all aspects of a college dormitory. Supervised residents, kitchen and maintenance staff. Served as a liaison to the Student Affairs Office.
Other Experience:	Groundskeeper, House Painter, Waitress

REFERENCES AVAILABLE

Terri Franks
15 Nob Hill
San Francisco, CA 91405

Job Objective

Graphic Designer

Work Experience

TERRI FRANKS DESIGN, San Francisco, CA
Freelance Designer, 1996 to Present
- *Design brochures, ads, posters*
- *Coordinate design details for fashion shows*

BERKELEY COLLEGE OF DESIGN, Berkeley, CA
Graphic Design Intern, 1995
- *Designed printed materials for university clients*
- *Finished projects included alumni directory and admissions brochure*

FERN LABS, Inc., Berkeley, CA
Graphics Assistant, 1994-1995
- *Designed and produced illustrations for brochures*

UNIVERSITY OF MINNESOTA, Minneapolis, MN
Photographer, 1992-1993
- *Took photos for university publications*

Education

Berkeley College of Design, Berkeley, CA
B.A. in Graphic Design, May 1997

University of Minnesota, Minneapolis, MN
B.A. in History, 1993

Awards

Northern California Photography Exhibit: Third Place, 1996
Berkeley Student Design Show, Honorable Mention, 1997

References

Available on Request

JOHN MARUM
489 McCauley
Oakland, CA 94609
415/555-7020

Objective:	Social work position utilizing my experience with youth programs, substance abuse recovery, and/or inmate rehabilitation.
Education:	M.S.W., 1995 Stanford University, Palo Alto, CA B.A. in English, 1992 University of Chicago, Chicago, IL
Coursework:	Introduction to Psychology Social Welfare Systems Theory of Social Work Abnormal Psychology Urban Problems Case Analysis History of Social Welfare Business Management Topics in Sociology
Field Work:	Counselor, 1996-Present Covenant House, Oakland, CA Interviewer, 1995-1996 Oakland Drug Rehab Program, Oakland, CA Volunteer, 1990-1991 San Francisco Youth Center, San Francisco, CA
References:	Furnished on request

DONALD PAPERMAN
303 13th Street
San Francisco, CA 94114
415/555-4311

EDUCATION

San Francisco State University, San Francisco, CA
B.A. in Communications, expected June 1998
Current G.P.A. of 3.36
Dean's List

COURSES

Journalism	Broadcasting
Mass Communications	Public Relations
Film	Child Psychology
Human Behavior	Sociology
English Literature	Child Welfare

WORK EXPERIENCE

Gamma Gamma Phi, Evanston, IL
Public Relations Assistant, 1996 to Present
Handle press releases and contacts with chapter members.
Help to establish new branch chapters.

HONORS

Panda Scholarship
Dean's List
Communications Honor Society
Gamma Gamma Phi

REFERENCES

Available on request

LUIS CASTILLO
8155 N. KNOX
SKOKIE, IL 60076
708/555-3168

JOB OBJECTIVE: Sales position where I can utilize my retail sales, cash
management, and supervisory skills

WORK EXPERIENCE:

Gateway, Inc., Chicago, IL
Manager/Salesperson, 11/96 - Present

Manage own jewelry business. Sell jewelry at wholesale and retail levels. Negotiate
prices with customers. Handle all finances and bookkeeping.

West Miami Jewelry, Miami, FL
Manager, 1/93 - 11/96

Managed a retail jewelry store. Oversaw all aspects of sales, purchasing, and
bookkeeping. Supervised two employees.

EDUCATION:

Interamerica Business Institute, Chicago, IL 2/97 - present
Major: Business Management

Northeastern University, Chicago, IL
Attended 1991- 1993
Area of concentration: Business Management

References available on request.

PAMELA SUE HUSPERS

Permanent Address: Temporary Address:
South East Hollow Road   150 Ft. Washington Ave.
Berlin, NY 10951   New York, NY 10032
(518) 555-6057   (212) 555-8934

OBJECTIVE: A management trainee position in the telecommunications industry.

EDUCATION: Bachelor of Science, Communications
                    New York University, New York, NY
                    Date of Graduation, May 1997
                    Communications G.P.A. 3.8
                    Academic G.P.A. 3.5

PROFESSIONAL
EXPERIENCE: **Tutor, Self-employed, September 1996 - Present**
                    Help students to better understand the basic concepts of mathematics.

                    Tax Consultant, V.I.T.A. (Volunteer Income Tax Assistance), Spring 1997
                    Provided income tax assistance to lower income and elderly taxpayers who were
                    unable to prepare returns or pay for professional assistance.

                    Cook, Randy's Seafood, New York, NY, Summer 1996
                    Prepared and cooked assorted seafood dishes. Accounted for deliveries and
                    receiving.

                    **General Laborer and Driver, Jones Construction, Brooklyn, NY,
                    Summers, 1994 and 1995**
                    Operated heavy machinery and handled other aspects of my job including
                    delivering materials to and from various job sites.

ACTIVITIES
AND HONORS: Beta Alpha Psi (Communications Honor Society), 1996-1997
                    Dean's List, three semesters
                    A.I.S.E.C. - Association for International Business
                    Racquetball and tennis teams

REFERENCES: Available upon request

YOLANDA FINKELSTEIN
54444 S. MAGNOLIA
NORTH HOLLYWOOD, CA 90042
818/555-2909
818/555-2789

CAREER OBJECTIVE

Interior Design and Decorative Arts

SKILLS

*Creative floor plans

*Functional design details

*Coordinated fabrics and furnishings

*Personalized color schemes and textiles designs

EMPLOYMENT HISTORY

Magnolia Street Design Studio
Owner
1996-Present

Madigan Textiles
Student Intern
1994-1996

EDUCATION

University of California
B.A. in Decorative Arts
Awarded June 1996

REFERENCES

Client list, portfolio, and references are available.

■■■

Theonios Petropolus
8900 Santa Monica Blvd. #802
Los Angles, CA 90069
Tel. 213/555-4098
Web site: www.****.com

GOAL: Programmer/analyst position with opportunity to
develop skills in software design.

SKILLS: CICS, OS2, COBOL II, FileAid, OS/MVS, EASYTRIEVE,
Data Ease, INFOSWITCH, VSAM, TSO/ISPF, FALCON.

EXPERIENCE: **Colonial Insurance**
Programmer
8/97 to Present

Accomplishments:
~Developed mainframe programs to create a download file
for pension administration package.
~Converted and maintained the raw material paper inventory system that
tracked $9M paper inventory, from a Honeywell DPS-88 platform
to an IBM.

Williams Financial Group
Programmer
6/96 to 8/97

Accomplishments:
~As programmer and project manager for wholesale financial
core, developed front-end processor to reformat invoice information
into trust finance agreements using multiple IMS databases.

EDUCATION: BOSTON COLLEGE, Bachelor of Science Degree, June 1996
MAJOR: Finance
MINOR: Computer and Information Services

REFERENCES: Personal and professional references available.

MARK E. RUCZINSKI
4330 Chesapeake N.W.
Washington, DC 20010
202/555-1331

CAREER GOAL: Attorney for a mid to large-sized
                    law firm.

EDUCATION: Pace University
                    White Plains, NY
                    J.D., June 1997

                    Iona College
                    Rochelle, NY
                    M.B.A., June 1994
                    B.A., June 1992

PROFESSIONAL
QUALIFICATIONS: Admission to New York Bar, 1997
                    Certified Public Accountant, New York, 1994
                    Member of the American Institute of CPAs
                    Member of the New York Society of CPAs

BUSINESS
EXPERIENCE: **Greyhound Bus Lines, New York, NY**
                    Assistant General Counsel and
                    Assistant to Treasurer
                    1995 to Present

                    Handle tax research and planning for the
                    corporation and its subsidiaries. Conduct
                    legal research.

                    City of Washington, Department of Finance
                    Assistant to Financial Analyst
                    1994 to 1995

                    Assisted with financial analysis and
                    preparation of financial reports, including
                    the annual financial report and financial
                    schedules for bond prospectus.

                    References submitted upon request

JOHN LEE
3310 15th Street
San Francisco, CA 94114
415/555-1687

PROFESSIONAL
OBJECTIVE: An entry-level position in the field of accounting leading to managerial
responsibilities.

EDUCATION: SAN FRANCISCO STATE UNIVERSITY, San Francisco, CA
Master of Science, May 1997
Major: Accounting

Program included independent study of Advanced Accounting Theory,
Financial Statement Analysis, and Tax Law.

G.P.A.: 3.5/4.0

Thesis: Impacts of Economic Recovery

STANFORD UNIVERSITY, Palo Alto, CA
Bachelor of Science, June 1995
Major: Business

WORK
EXPERIENCE: MAY CO., San Francisco, CA
Department Manager, Men's Clothing, 1995-Present

Supervise sales staff. Manage shipment and cash management
responsibilities. Create sales analysis reports for use by management
and buyers.

REFERENCES AVAILABLE

HARRIET SCHUMACHER

1414 N. Montebello Drive
Berkeley, CA 98028
415/555-4930

EDUCATION: University of California at Berkeley
                        Bachelor of Science in Journalism
                        Expected June 1998

HONORS: Beta Gamma Epsilon Honorary Society
                        Dean's List
                        Manley Writing Award, 1997

ACTIVITIES: Treasurer, Gamma Gamma Gamma Sorority
                        Resident Advisor
                        Homecoming Planning Committee
                        Alumni Welcoming Committee

**WORK
EXPERIENCE:**   Berkeley Dispatch
                        Student Intern, 1996 to Present

                        Assisted in layout, editing, and reporting for local newspaper.
                        Wrote and edited articles. Handled preparatory research for
                        local sports events.

                        University of California at Berkeley
                        Office Assistant, Journalism School, 1994 to 1996
                        Assisted with registrations, filing, and typing. Arranged
                        application materials. Assembled course packs.

SPECIAL SKILLS: Fluent in German. Hands-on computer experience using
                        LOTUS 1-2-3 and dBASE III.

REFERENCES: Available on request.

CHRISTOPHER BERNARD SMALLS
600 W. Porter Street, # 5
Las Vegas, NV 89890
514/555-3893

OBJECTIVE

A position as a management trainee in a manufacturing company.

EDUCATION

University of Nevada, Las Vegas, NV
Bachelor of Science in Business
Expected June 1998

HONORS

Dean's List for four semesters
Dornburn Scholarship
U.N.L.V. Undergraduate Business Award

WORK EXPERIENCE

Porter Rand & Associates, Seattle, WA
Sales Intern, 1997
Assisted sales staff in the areas of research, demographics, sales forecasts, identifying new customers, and promotion.

University of Nevada, Las Vegas, NV
Research/Office Assistant, 1995-1996
Researched and compiled materials for department professors. Arranged filing system and supervisor's library. Organized department inventory.

SPECIAL SKILLS

Experience using IBM and Apple hardware and WordPerfect 6.0 and dBASE III software programs.

JANE WIGGINS

1814 N. Seminola Ave., #2442
Cleveland, OH 47889
216/555-3400 (Daytime)
216/555-2910 (Evenings)

CAREER OBJECTIVE

To become a sales representative for an office supplies manufacturer.

EMPLOYMENT HISTORY

Tempo Office Supply Co., Cleveland, OH
Executive Secretary to Sales Manager, 1996 - Present

Assisted the sales manager in various office activities and procedures. Handled price quotations, information
on product line, customer inquiries on shipments, and special orders. Arranged travel and transportation, hotel,
and scheduling of seminars and meetings. Drafted monthly reports on sales procedures and profit margins.
Managed computerization of the office records.

James Plastics, St. Louis, MO
Secretary to Manager of Publications, 1990 - 1993

Arranged conferences for the department. Dealt directly with staff members in a variety of manners including
routing editing duties and proofreading responsibilities. Edited and proofread interoffice memos and a weekly
department newsletter. Arranged for printing and distribution. Supervised two student interns.

EDUCATION

Cleveland University, Cleveland, OH
B.S. in Marketing, 1997 (Evening Division)

St. Louis School of Business, St. Louis, MO
Completed advanced secretarial course, 1990

SPECIAL SKILLS

Proficiency on IBM and COMPAQ hardware and WordPerfect 6.0, DISPLAYWRITE and MULTIMATE
software.
Knowledge of Spanish.

REFERENCES

Available on request

CARRINE KANKA
9370 Trent Drive
Jackson, MS 73127

609/555-2909
609/555-3898

JOB OBJECTIVE

Position that allows me to use my writing and editorial skill to promote environmental awareness.

SKILLS AND ACCOMPLISHMENTS

--Edited Save The Planet, an environmental publication directed at concerned citizens.

--Wrote articles for Conservation magazine.

--Wrote technical articles and instructional manuals on software applications, office equipment, and kitchen appliances.

--Edited grant proposals for a local college.

EMPLOYMENT HISTORY

Freelance Writer, 1996 - Present

EDUCATION

Columbia University, Columbia, SC
B.A. in Journalism, June 1997
Minor in History

SPECIAL SKILLS

Knowledge of WordPerfect 6.0, PageMaker, and QuarkXPress
Working knowledge of French and German.

REFERENCES AND WRITING SAMPLES AVAILABLE

MARTIN C. CHAN
64 Collin Road
Miami, FL 30392
(305) 555-7757

GOAL: Production Assistant for Film Company

EXPERIENCE: Location scouting
                Securing film permits
                Locating and managing props
                Handling travel arrangements for crews
                Supervising extras on location
                Assisting producers, location managers
                Photographing promotional stills

EMPLOYERS: NEW ORDER PRODUCTIONS, Miami, FL
                Production Assistant, 1997-Present

                TERT FILM PRODUCTIONS, Chicago, IL
                Production Coordinator, Summer 1997

                BALTIMORE FILM FESTIVAL, Baltimore, MD
                Production Assistant, Summer 1996

                KKSF RADIO, Berkeley, CA
                Producer, 1993-1997

EDUCATION: UNIVERSITY OF CALIFORNIA, Berkeley, CA
                B.A. in Film Production, 1997

                   REFERENCES ON REQUEST

PETER THOMASSON
Fulton Hall
2300 East Harrison
Room 306
Chicago, IL 60633

312/555-4849

OBJECTIVE: A career in the field of finance.

EDUCATION: University of Illinois at Chicago, Chicago, IL
Bachelor of Arts in Economics expected June 1998

HONORS: Phi Beta Kappa
Dean's list five times
Robeson Business Scholarship, 1997

ACTIVITIES: Vice President, Beta Gamma Fraternity
Teaching Assistant, Accounting Department
Homecoming Planning Committee
Baseball Team
Student Rights Group

**WORK
EXPERIENCE:**   IBM, Northbrook, IL
Accounting Intern, 1996

Assisted finance department in the areas of computer accounting, bookkeeping, financial statements, forecasts, and planning. Extensive use of spreadsheet software programs.

University of Illinois at Chicago, Chicago, IL
Office Assistant, Journalism School, 1995

Assisted with registrations, filing, and typing. Arranged application materials. Prepared course materials for faculty.

SPECIAL SKILLS: Hands-on computer experience using Lotus 1-2-3 and dBASE III.

REFERENCES: Available on request.

RANDALL TURNER

698 4th St.
Atlanta, Georgia 30356
770/555-1212

GOAL: Bookkeeper

SKILLS: *Handled accounts payable and receivable.
                 *Kept ledger records.
                 *Assisted with budget forecasting.
                 *Calculated payroll deductions.
                 *Prepared periodic statements.
                 *Produced invoices.
                 *Supervised annual inventory.

EXPERIENCE: University of Tennessee, Memphis, TN
                 Bookkeeper, Campus Booksellers, 1996 - Present

                 Henderson, Inc., Memphis, TN
                 Clerk/Finance Dept., Summers 1996 - 1997

EDUCATION: Georgia State University, Atlanta, GA
                 B.S. in Finance, expected May 1998

REFERENCES: Available on request

LAWRENCE OATES
102 Maple St.
Louisville, KY 94229

502/555-4792

CAREER GOAL: A technical position in the field of Electrical Engineering.

EDUCATION: **University of Louisville,** Louisville, KY
B.S. Electrical Engineering expected June 1998
G.P.A. 3.56

SKILLS: Experience with DPL and Pascal. Use of Unix,
Wylbur and Executive Operating Systems. Knowledge of SPICE.

WORK
EXPERIENCE: **Nichols Technical, Inc.,** Memphis, TN
Technical Assistant, Summer 1997

Handled warehouse inspections, trend analyses and programming.
Involved with statistics and parts engineering groups.

ACTIVITIES: EE Club
President, Delta Upsilon Fraternity

REFERENCES: Available upon request

MARY E. MARLOW

4455 W. Gunderson Street
Berkeley, CA 91404
(415) 555-4909

GOAL:

Labor and delivery staff R.N. position, with opportunity
to develop neonatal intensive care skills.

CREDENTIALS:

B.S.N., McAdams College, Berkeley, CA

California Nursing License #975-987436

C.P.R. and P.A.L.S. Certified

Member, California Nursing Association

EXPERIENCE:

1997 to Present
Labor and Delivery Staff Nurse
Stevenson's Women's Hospital, Berkeley, CA

Evaluate and triage patients upon admission. Monitor
their progress. Teach self-care, pain management
techniques, breastfeeding, and infant care. Care for
healthy newborns in nursery. Arrange discharge planning.

ADDITIONAL
INFORMATION:

Excellent references available.

Willing to relocate.

Anna Castillo
4742 N. Lawndale
Chicago, IL 60625
312/555-2574

Objective

Children's Caseworker

Education

University of Illinois, Champaign, IL
B.S. in Social Work, June 1997
Minor: Psychology

Work Experience

Association House, Chicago, IL
Case Manager, August 1997 to Present

Provide social services to children, parents, and foster parents.
Visit and interview prospective foster parents.
Write case reports.

Memberships

Illinois Association of Social Workers
National Caseworkers Association

References

Submitted upon request

HAROLD C. JONES
609 Lincoln Road
Houston, Texas 77386
(713) 555-1947
www.http.****.com

OBJECTIVE

Computer Programming Position

EDUCATION

Baylor University
B.S. in Computer Science expected June 1998

Courses in COBOL, BASIC, RPG II, Pascal, and C

G.P.A. of 3.9/4.0

Earned 50% of tuition by working while carrying a full
course load.

EMPLOYMENT

1996 to Present
Computer Lab Assistant
Baylor University

Instruct undergraduates in the use of computer hardware and software. Assistance ranges from word-
processing instruction to programming assignments.

Summers, 1994 and 1995
Sales Associate
Computer World

Sold computer equipment and software. Answered
customers' questions. Provided ongoing customer
service and training.

REFERENCES

Available

BELINDA FERNANDEZ

7 S. Industrial Parkway
Hilo, HI 98191

808/555-5401
808/555-8032

EDUCATION

M.B.A. in Marketing
University of Hawaii, Hilo, HI
Degree awarded June 1997

B.S. in Finance
University of Colorado, Boulder, CO
Degree awarded May 1995

Courses included:

Sales & Marketing	Tax Law
Business Law	Sociology
Consumer Behavior	Mass Marketing
Mass Communications	Calculus
Advertising	Sales Management
Statistics	

HONORS

Summa Cum Laude, 1995
Dean's List, 1994, 1995

WORK HISTORY

PACIFIC DEVELOPMENT CORPORATION, Hilo, HI

8/97 to Present	Administrative Assistant/Sales Department
	Handle billing, inventory, public relations, correspondence.
Summer 1996	Sales Trainee
	Assisted with billing, orders, shipping, and inventory.

JAMES ROBERT WEITSMA

1200 Wodler Drive
Apartment 3E
Chicago, IL 60607
Telephone: 312/555-4903

OBJECTIVE:	A position as a sales management trainee.
EDUCATION:	NORTHWESTERN UNIVERSITY, Evanston, IL

B.A. in Advertising, expected June 1998
Dean's List five quarters
3.6 G.P.A. in major field
3.5 G.P.A. overall

Activities:
Alumni Committee
Student Activities Board

WORK EXPERIENCE:

AT&T, Chicago, IL
Sales Intern, 9/97 to Present
Assist sales manager in areas of promotion, product development, and marketing.

HANDELMAN MARKETING, Winnetka, IL
Telephone Surveyor, Summer 1996

YESTERDAY'S, Evanston, IL
Waiter, Summer 1995

SPECIAL SKILLS:

Fluent in Spanish.
Familiar with WordPerfect 6.0, ClarisWorks, and Lotus 1-2-3

REFERENCES: Available on request

R O B E R T   M U L L E T T

339 S. Jordan Street
Shreveport, LA 22909
(318) 555-3893

Objective:	A career in environmental testing
Education:	M.S. in Atmospheric Science, June 1997 North Carolina State University Raleigh, NC B.S. in Chemistry, June 1995 Shreveport College Shreveport, LA
Experience:	Wexler Corporation, Shreveport, LA

Experience:

Wexler Corporation, Shreveport, LA
Position: Lab Chemist
Dates: 8/97 to Present
Duties: Analysis of chemical content in
                  building materials to comply with
                  OSHA regulations.

North Carolina State University, Raleigh, NC
Position: Research Assistant
Dates: 9/96 to 6/97
Duties: Dispersion modeling of fugitive
                  process emissions from manufacturing
                  operations such as plastic pipe
                  extrusion and injection molding.

References: Available

SAM GARRISON
83 Main Place #3B
Portland, ME 04129
207/555-2321

OBJECTIVE: A position as an advertising assistant where I can use my advertising, marketing, and graphic arts skills.

EDUCATION: University of Maine, New Brunswick, ME
B.A. in Advertising, expected June 1998
Major Fields: Advertising, Marketing, Graphic Arts, Journalism, Business

HONORS: Dean's List
Worthington Academic Merit Scholarship

**WORK
EXPERIENCE:**   Lee J. Harris, Inc., Bangor, ME
Advertising Intern, Summer 1997
Handled four accounts for advertising agency. Designed and laid out ads.
Wrote copy. Assisted with traffic control. Served as intermediary between client
and account executives.

Bangor Life Magazine, Bangor, ME
Advertising Assistant, part-time, 1996
Assisted in designing ads for magazine copy. Gained experience with Adobe Illustrator
and Adobe Photoshop programs. Provided basic pricing and design information
to clients.

New Brunswick Daily, New Brunswick, ME
Freelance writer, 1994 to 1996
Wrote feature articles on local community news, including education, sports, politics,
and the arts. Provided photos and illustrations in support of various articles.

REFERENCES: References and portfolio are available.

SONDRA NIKE
1500 W. Redwood Drive
Salt Lake City, UT 83902

801/555-3921

OVERVIEW

Strong computer and organizational skills and knowledge
of the travel industry. Enjoy fast-paced work environment.
Excellent interpersonal and communications skills. Interested
in full-time travel agent position.

EDUCATION

Salt Lake Community College
Certified Travel Agent, September 1997

Central High School
Diploma Awarded, June 1997

EXPERIENCE

Harper Street Travel Agency
Part-Time Reservationist
July 1997 to Present

SKILLS

WordPerfect 6.0
Lotus 1-2-3

Fluent in Spanish

Typing speed of 60 words per minute

References Are Available

WILLIAM GAVIN

2666 Western Ave. #44
Madison, WI 55590
414/555-2029

<u>Career Goal:</u>	Accounting
<u>Education:</u>	UNIVERSITY OF WISCONSIN, Madison, WI M.B.A., June 1997 Area of Concentration: Accounting UNIVERSITY OF CHICAGO, Chicago, IL B.A. in History, May 1995 Triton Honorary Society Leopold Scholarship
<u>Areas of Study:</u>	Basic, Intermediate, and Advanced Accounting Business Law Cost Accounting Statistical Methods Planning and Control Tax Law Investments
<u>Work History:</u>	WISCONSIN FEDERAL, Madison, WI Trainee Examiner, 1997 to Present Participate in test audits, preparation of schedules of earnings, audits of expenses and capital accounts, and classification and appraisal of assets.

REFERENCES AVAILABLE

SANDRA TRESVANT
33 N. Main St. Fargo, ND 58102
701/555-7310

GOAL

Legal Assistant for a medium to large-sized law firm.

EDUCATION

Stevenson College, Fargo, ND
A.A. degree expected June 1998
Major: Legal Assisting Technology

Coursework includes

Tort and Insurance Law and Claims Investigation
Contracts, Sales, and Secured Transactions
Landlord and Tenant Mediation
Law Office Practice and Procedure
Wills and Trusts

EMPLOYMENT HISTORY

Prudential Insurance Company, Fargo, ND
Office Assistant, Sept. 1997 - Present
Handle general office duties. Take and transcribe dictation
for sales staff. Typing, filing, phones.

Barker Company, Fargo, ND
Secretary, June 1996 - Sept. 1997
Provided information to customers. Answered phones.
Typed and processed orders.

References on Request

WILLIAM PERRIS MONDAY

606 W. Washington, #1B
Chicago, IL 60657
312/555-1201

EDUCATION

ROOSEVELT UNIVERSITY, Chicago, IL
B.A. in Accounting, June 1997

EXPERIENCE

CITY OF CHICAGO, Chicago, IL
Finance Assistant, Department of Housing
Summer 1996

- Evaluated accounts and operations for compliance with department procedures and policies.
- Assembled charts and tables.
- Examined fiscal records and operating procedures.
- Prepared audit reports.

MCCAULEY, INC., Indianapolis, IN
Assistant, Accounting Department
Summer 1995

- Maintained books of original entry, trial balance and general ledger.
- Prepared financial statements.
- Assisted with bank transactions, settlements and adjustments.

REFERENCES FURNISHED UPON REQUEST

BARRY SCRANT

111 Willoughby Road #3
Parkview, SD 30039
605/555-2212

OBJECTIVE

A job in personnel administration leading to personnel management.

EDUCATION

Jefferson University, Parkview, SD
B.A. in Sociology, expected June 1998

Areas of concentration: employee relations, psychology, communications.

SKILLS & EXPERIENCE

Interviewed fifty South Dakota farmers for senior research project,
The South Dakota Farm Industry: Boom or Bust? Collected and
analyzed data. Developed a questionnaire.

Served as a student representative on the university's planning
committee. Worked on a subcommittee that dealt with policy formulation.

Wrote the article "South Dakota's Future" for South Dakota News,
October 1996.

Collected and analyzed statistical data on local Farm Union elections.

References provided on request

EMMY DANO
1600 Roberts Street
Oakland, CA 92112
415/555-4155

Career Objective

> A position as an insurance underwriter.

Education

> Parker College, Andover, MD
> B.S. in Marketing, June 1997
>
> Honors:
> G.P.A. 3.5
> Harrison McDonald Scholarship Winner
> Voted Outstanding Senior by Marketing Department

Work Experience

> E. Katsulos Associates, Andover, MD
> 1997- Present
>
> Accomplishments: Hired as junior insurance investigator and promoted to assistant claims representative within six months. Voted Employee of the Month in September 1997. Received favorable evaluation and was commended for discovering fraudulent health care claims through investigation in the field.

References

> Provided on request

| SANTI | 4390 S. Finley | 504/555-3903 |
| NOLE | Baton Rouge, LA 20932 | 504/555-3892 |

CAREER OBJECTIVE

Graphic Design

EDUCATION

University of Louisiana, Baton Rouge, LA
B.A. in Commercial Art, expected June 1998

EXPERIENCE

Baton Graphics, Baton Rouge, LA
Intern, Summer 1997

University of Louisiana, Baton Rouge, LA
Yearbook Art Director, 1996

Emerge Magazine
Visual Art Editor, 1995

MEMBERSHIPS

Art Directors and Artists Club, 1996 to Present

AWARDS

University of Louisiana Student Design Competition, First Place, May 1996

REFERENCES

References and portfolio available for review.

GAVIN T. SIMPKINS

222 Handlebar Ave.
Amarillo, TX 78811
806/555-8280

OBJECTIVE: Machinist

EDUCATION: AMARILLO TECHNICAL COLLEGE, Amarillo, TX
                  A.S. Degree in Machine Shop, June 1997

COURSEWORK: Machine Shop
                  Fundamentals of Metallurgy
                  Drafting
                  Basics of Manufacturing
                  Technical Math
                  Welding
                  Introduction to Numerical Control

SKILLS: Drill Presses, Lathes, Grinding, Mills

WORK
EXPERIENCE: FARGO PACKING CO., Plainview, TX
                  Maintenance Worker, 1996 - 1997

                  Handled maintenance of company vehicles and heavy machinery.
                  Parked and operated company trucks.

REFERENCES: Available on request

RONETTE TAWANA JOHNSON

1750 N. Normandie Ave. #201
Miami, FL 33505
305/555-2922 (Home)
305/555-4000 (Office)

OBJECTIVE: A position at a commercial radio station.

SKILLS AND ACCOMPLISHMENTS:

*Assisted in the management of a college radio station.

*Helped to direct and supervise staff.

*Established music format guidelines.

*Wrote and edited budget proposals.

*Assisted in financial matters.

*Created and implemented new music format.

*Served as on-air personality.

*Trained a staff of disc jockeys.

EMPLOYMENT HISTORY:

WLVE-RADIO, Ft. Lauderdale, FL
Assistant General Manager, 1997 - Present

WRDO-RADIO, Ft. Myers, FL
Music Director, 1996 - 1997

WWOP-TV, New York, NY
Student Intern, Summer 1995

EDUCATION:

UNIVERSITY OF SOUTH FLORIDA, Ft. Lauderdale, FL
B.A. in Broadcasting, June 1997

FT. MYERS COLLEGE, Ft. Myers, FL 1993 - 1995

Mary Lynn Bademacher
250 N. Brady Street
Cleveland, Ohio

(216) 555-6906

Background: *Recently licensed electrician seeking a full-time position doing commercial, industrial, or residential electrical work.*

Credentials: *Ohio License #C-57488*

Certified by Cleveland Technical College Apprenticeship Program, June 1997

Employers: *DiAngelo Company*
June 1997 to Present

Responsible for a variety of commercial and industrial wiring projects. Interact with architects, contractors, subcontractors, and building inspectors. Excellent record of completing projects at or below projected costs, while complying to codes and meeting deadlines.

References: *Michael DiAngelo, Owner*
DiAngelo Company
(216) 555-6958 Ext. 399

Eliza Sullivan, Director
Cleveland Technical College Apprenticeship Program
(216) 555-3932

Renee C. Caldwell
6500 Riverside Drive #422
Washington, D.C. 01991

202-555-5594

Objective: Administrative Assistant

Education: Jefferson City College, Washington, D.C.
A.A.   Office Administration and Technology
Date of Graduation: June 1997

Skills: Knowledge of WordPerfect 6.0, Lotus 1-2-3, and ClarisWorks
Typing Speed of 65 words per minute
Excellent written and oral communication skills

Experience: Adley Manufacturing, Washington, D.C.
Administrative Assistant/Receptionist
June 1997 to Present
Manage switchboard and front desk for midsize manufacturing
firm. Duties include greeting clients, answering and routing all
incoming calls, producing correspondence.

References: Submitted on request.

JOHNNY KAZELL
5320 Wilshire Blvd.
Los Angeles, CA 90069
213/555-9282

OBJECTIVE: Seeking a marketing position in the music industry.

WORK
EXPERIENCE: Hit Productions, Los Angeles, CA
Public Relations/Marketing Assistant, 5/97 - Present

Assist P.R. Director with all duties, including radio promotion
and retail marketing. Coordinate radio and print interviews for
artists. Typing, filing, and answering phones.

KCLA Radio, Los Angeles, CA
Music Director, 6/96 - 5/97

Selected appropriate music for student radio station. Oversaw
daily operations of music library and programming department.
Supervised staff of six student volunteers.

EDUCATION: UCLA, Los Angeles, CA
B.A. in Arts Management, May 1997

ACTIVITIES: Phi Mu Alpha Music Fraternity, President
Alpha Lambda Fraternity

SPECIAL
SKILLS: Working knowledge of Microsoft Word and Lotus 1-2-3.

References available on request.

Shirley G. Browne
2552 Harrod Lane
Boulder, CO 80304
303/555-4849

Goal:	R.N. Position
Experience:	1996 to Present
Volunteer Nursing Assistant
Mercy Hospice

Assist nursing staff in providing primary care to terminally ill patients. Monitor patients' status and vital signs and report to nursing supervisor. Provide grooming and bathing assistance and emotional support for patients.

1994 to 1996
Medical Records Clerk
Bishop Hospital

Recorded patient histories and insurance information. Maintained computerized patient database. Gained extensive knowledge of medical terminology. |
| Education: | Bishop Hospital School of Nursing
R.N. expected June 1998 |
| Credentials: | C.P.R. certified
Member, American Student Nurses Association |
| References: | Available |

ADRIENNA DYSON

5 Oak Avenue #2
Crescent City, MO 60166
816/555-8161

JOB OBJECTIVE:	Early childhood education/day care.
EDUCATION:	SOUTH MISSOURI STATE COLLEGE, Springfield, MO B.A. in Early Childhood Education, expected June 1998
COURSEWORK:	Early Childhood Education Psychology of Learning History of Childhood Problems The Urban Family The Exceptional Child
WORK HISTORY:	SOUTH MISSOURI STATE COLLEGE, Springfield, MO Day Care Director, 1995 to Present Supervise day care services for the children of faculty members. Interview, select, and oversee student workers. SOUTHMALL DAY CARE, Springfield, IL Teacher's Assistant, 1992 to 1994 Assisted with play sessions, outdoor activities, and learning games. Met with parents regarding their child's progress.

REFERENCES PROVIDED ON REQUEST

CAROL PAGE

500 E. Maple Street, Apt. #4
Eugene, OR 97412
503/555-4122

CAREER OBJECTIVE: Librarian

EDUCATION: University of Oregon, Eugene, OR
                       M.S. in Library Science
                       Degree Expected June 1998

                       University of Mississippi,
                       Oxford, MS
                       B.S. in Linguistics, May 1996

WORK EXPERIENCE: Eugene Public Library, Eugene, OR
                       Internship, 1996-1997

                       Conducted research. Maintained and
                       updated files. Assisted in the
                       acquisition of new books. Organized
                       and stocked audiovisual materials.

                       Oxford Public Library, Oxford, MS
                       Assistant to Children's Librarian,
                       1994-1995

                       Developed reading programs for grade
                       school children. Taught children the
                       use of reference section and computer
                       catalog. Acquired new books and
                       magazines.

REFERENCES: Available

ELIZABETH PERLMAN
233 Sandler Road
Los Angeles, CA
213/555-3284

GOAL

Career as a floral designer.

EDUCATION

Los Angeles City College, Los Angeles, CA
Certificate of Completion, June 1997
Ornamental Horticulture Program

SKILLS

- Floral Design: excellent understanding of floral arranging, plant care and selection
- Sales: experience with diverse customer base including corporate clients
- Cash Management Skills: comfortable operating cash register
- Marketing: able to develop marketing strategies to increase sales

WORK HISTORY

6/97 to Present
Freelance Floral Designer

Design and sell dried floral arrangements for special occasions, especially weddings. Specialize in large arrangements and bridal bouquets. Purchase materials, create and personally deliver all items.

Accomplishments:

- Increased business by 20% during the last year.
- Initiated cooperative marketing arrangement with two area photographers and a caterer that has led to an increase in business for all participants.
- Recently featured in *LA Living* magazine.

REFERENCES AVAILABLE

JOANN BIANCHI
7282 56th St.
Richmond, CA 98993
415/555-8083

OBJECTIVE: Personnel Management

WORK EXPERIENCE:

>   Avery Publishing Company, San Francisco, CA
>   Payroll Specialist, 9/96 - present
>
>   Determine job grading system. Evaluate jobs. Maintain employee budget. Conduct performance
>   appraisals. Decide wage increases and adjustments. Set salary ranges. Write job descriptions.
>   Coordinate compensation surveys. Gather data on vacations, sick time, and leaves of absence.

EDUCATION:

>   University of California at Santa Barbara
>   Bachelor's Degree in Economics, May 1996
>
>   Personnel Management Institute
>   Harrison University, Seattle, WA
>   Summer 1996

HONORS:

>   U.C.S.B. Economics Scholarship, 1994-1996
>   Elected Student Government Treasurer, 1994
>   Gamma Kappa Phi Honorary Society, 1994-1996

REFERENCES:

>   Available upon request

GEORGE COLGAN
1711 N. GURMAN AVE.
ATLANTIC CITY, NJ 02110

609/555-8971

CAREER OBJECTIVE: Restaurant Management

EXPERIENCE:

Food Service
- Supervised kitchen staff of eight.
- Conducted business with a local catering service.
- Interviewed, hired, and trained student food service workers.
- Catered banquets.
- Served dining patrons as a waiter.

Management

- Planned budget and strictly adhered to it.
- Organized work schedules for student workers.
- Managed purchasing, bookkeeping, and payroll.

Food Preparation

- Assisted in the preparation of meals for 90 children and adults at a summer camp.
- Planned meals for 250 resident students.

EMPLOYMENT HISTORY:

Szabo Food Service/Jersey College, Atlantic City, NJ
Food Service Director, 1997 - present

Jersey College, Atlantic City, NJ
Assistant Cafeteria Director, 1996 - 1997

North Shore Children's Camp, Skokie, IL
Dining Hall Director, 1995 - 1996

Paco's Restaurant, Atlantic City, NJ
Waiter, 1994

EDUCATION:

Jersey College, Atlantic City, NJ
B.S. in Business, expected June 1998

YOORI MATSUKA

2300 East Harrison
Apartment 306
Chicago, IL 60633
312/555-4849

~Professional Respiratory Therapist~

SKILLS:

- Respiratory Therapy
- Pulmonary Function Studies
- EKG Testing
- Stress Testing
- CPR Instruction
- Patient Education

WORK HISTORY:

St. Jude's Medical Center
Respiratory Therapy Technician
1997 to Present

Red Cross
Part-Time CPR Instructor
1996 to Present

EDUCATION:

New Haven Junior College
Associate's Degree
Respiratory Therapy, December 1996

REFERENCES:

Available on Request.

JEFFERY P. STOUT
14-44 E. Tyrone Ave.
Omaha, NE 49940
402/555-3210

OBJECTIVE: Business Management

EDUCATION: UNIVERSITY OF NEBRASKA, Omaha, NE
                          M.B.A. expected June 1998
                          Area of Concentration: Financial Management/Accounting

                          SHREVEPORT COLLEGE, Shreveport, LA
                          B.A. received June 1996
                          Major: Economics
                          Minor: Political Science

WORK HISTORY: **UNIVERSITY OF NEBRASKA, Omaha, NE**
                          Analytical Studies Intern, 8/97 to Present
                          Duties: Collect and organize data for university finance
                          studies. Conduct library research. Edit final drafts of
                          reports.

                          SHREVEPORT COLLEGE, Shreveport, LA
                          Resident Hall Assistant, 9/95 to 6/96
                          Duties: Oversaw all aspects of college dormitory.
                          Supervised residents, kitchen and maintenance staff. Served
                          as a liaison to the Student Affairs Office.

REFERENCES: On Request

FRED SCHNEIDER

9332 Hollywood Ave.
Camden, NJ 08630

609/555-9599

OBJECTIVE: Attorney

EDUCATION: PHILADELPHIA COLLEGE, Philadelphia, PA
Juris Doctor, June 1997

TULANE UNIVERSITY, New Orleans, LA
B.A., June 1994
Major: English Literature

COURSEWORK:

Contracts	Criminal Law
Wills & Trusts	Juvenile Law
Trial Practice	Corporate Law
Family Law	Tax Law
Insurance Law	Legal Research

**ACTIVITIES
& HONORS:**   Bently Scholarship
Junior Bar Association
Dean's List
Student Government Representative
Planning Committee
Baseball Team

REFERENCES: Available upon request.

EDWARD G. WILLIAMS

4114 Sergeant St. #3A
Cincinnati, OH 20999
601/555-1129

OBJECTIVE:	A career in the field of accounting.
EDUCATION:	CINCINNATI UNIVERSITY, Cincinnati, OH M.B.A., June 1996 Areas of Concentration: Accounting, Finance UNIVERSITY OF WISCONSIN, Madison, WI B.A. in Political Science, 1994 Morgan Scholarship
EMPLOYMENT:	BARTON & MORRIS, June 1996 to Present Junior Public Accountant Assist public accounting staff in conducting audits for clients. Review financial records and reports to judge their accuracy. Suggest management control procedures to enable clients to function efficiently and economically. Provide timely, accurate data to assist clients with sales and merger decisions.
ADDITIONAL INFORMATION:	C.P.A. received April 1997 Currently studying for Certified Internal Auditor Exam Member, National Society of Public Accountants
REFERENCES:	Available

JANIS JETER

777 Yorba Linda Ave.
Jacksonville,FL 22910
904/555-6164

GOAL: A position in manufacturing with opportunity for advancement

EDUCATION: **Parker Institute of Technology,** Jacksonville, FL
                         Bachelor of Science in Manufacturing Engineering Technology,
                         expected June 1998

                         Selected Coursework:

Work Measurement	Statistics
Manufacturing Analysis	Strength of Materials
Machine Design	Motion Analysis
Control Systems	Quality Assurance
Technical writing	Planning

EMPLOYMENT
HISTORY: **Wisconsin Manufacturing Co.,** Milwaukee, WI
                         Forklift Driver, Summers 1996, 1997
                         Drove forklifts. Repaired and serviced heavy machinery.

                         Penner Furniture, Inc., West Allis, WI
                         Warehouse Assistant, 1991-1993
                         Prepared furniture for delivery. Organized furniture stock.
                         Delivered furniture. Assisted in construction of furniture racks.

MEMBERSHIPS: Society of Manufacturing Engineers

REFERENCES: Submitted on request

JAMES SHU

55 Underland Park
Kalamazoo, MI 66666
616/555-5600
616/555-8818

CAREER GOAL: A job as a Medical Assistant

EDUCATION: Henderson Community College, Kalamazoo, MI
                     Medical Assistant Program
                     Certificate expected, June 1998

EXPERIENCE: Union Hospital, Kalamazoo, MI
                     Internship, August 1997 to Present

                     *Assist with medical exams and minor surgery.
                     *Handle routine lab procedures.
                     *Interview and schedule patients.
                     *Prepare patients for examination and x-rays.
                     *Sterilize instruments.
                     *Organize and maintain medical records.

MEMBERSHIPS: American Association of Medical Assistants

REFERENCES: Submitted upon request

JANIS DARIEN

345 W. 3rd St.   Telephone: 617/555-3291
Boston, MA 02210

JOB OBJECTIVE: To obtain a position as a marketing management trainee.

EDUCATION: Boston University, Boston, MA

B.A. degree in Economics, June 1997
Dean's list four quarters
3.5 GPA in major field
3.8 GPA overall

Plan to pursue graduate studies toward a
Master's degree in Marketing at Boston
University, Evening Division.

WORK EXPERIENCE: Lewis Advertising Agency, Boston, MA
Marketing Assistant, 9/97 to Present

Assist Marketing Manager in areas of promotion, product development
and demographic analysis.

Paterno Marketing, Boston, MA
Telephone Interviewer, Summer 1996

Conducted telemarketing surveys to help clients analyze demographics
and product demand and create marketing strategies.

SPECIAL SKILLS: Fluent in French.
Familiar with WordPerfect, ClarisWorks, Microsoft Works, Lotus1-2-3

REFERENCES: Available on request.

THELMA MARKS
418 Whitesburg Street
Wauconda, IL 60084

847-555-4949

Objective: Nurse Assistant Position

Overview: Nurse assistant experience working with geriatric clients in long-term care setting. Duties include monitoring and recording clients' vital signs, mood, appearance. Assist nursing staff in meeting clients' basic grooming, bathing, and nutrition needs. Take direction well while also advocating for patients as needed. Provide information and emotional support to clients and their families. Participate in care management conferences. Cooperate with nursing, physical therapy, and respiratory therapy personnel to develop comprehensive client care plans.

Prior experience in pediatric office setting. Duties included scheduling appointments, greeting patients, handling office phones, files, and correspondence.

Employers: Pinkerton Nursing Center, Wauconda, IL
6/97 to Present   Nurse Assistant

Kusler Medical Group, Deerfield, IL
4/95 to 6/97   Office Assistant

Education: Nursing Assistant Certification
Columbia College, Chicago, IL
June 1997

REFERENCES AVAILABLE

KIDS INC.

SERITA THOMAS
75 Crescent Lane
Birmingham, AL 22929
205-555-5059
www.******.com

Quality Day Care ~ Affordable Rates ~ Flexible Hours ~ Excellent References

CREDENTIALS: Alabama State University, Birmingham, AL
B.A. in Early Childhood Education
Minor: Psychology
Graduated June 1997

Courses:

Psychology of Learning
Early Childhood Education
History of Childhood
The Urban Family
The Exceptional Child

WORK HISTORY: June 1997 to Present
Owner/Operator of KIDS INC. Day Care

Provide quality day care from my home. Program
offers full-time, part-time, and drop-in services.
Emphasis is providing a safe and stimulating atmosphere
for preschool children.

May 1995 to June 1997
Teacher's Assistant
Birmingham University Day Care

Assisted director of university day care center in providing
games and learning activities for children of faculty and
staff.

WILLIAM HARRIS

P. O. Box 4112
Fargo, ND 52289
701/555-3930

OBJECTIVE

To obtain an entry-level position at a commercial radio station.

RADIO EXPERIENCE

WND-RADIO, Fargo, ND
ASSISTANT GENERAL MANAGER, 1996 - 1997

Assisted in the management of a student-run college radio station. Helped to direct and supervise a board of directors and an on-air staff to ensure efficient day-to-day operations. Established music format guidelines and made other management decisions. Wrote and edited budget proposals. Assisted in financial matters.

WND-RADIO, Fargo, ND
ALTERNATIVE MUSIC DIRECTOR, 1993 - 1996
Created and implemented station alternative music format. Managed, scheduled, and trained a staff of 15 on-air disc jockeys. Planned and organized club performances by local bands in conjunction with the station. Served as on-air personality.

EDUCATION

FARGO COLLEGE, Fargo, ND
B.S. in Business Administration, June 1997
Minor: Music

ACTIVITIES

Studio Engineer, 1994 - 1997
News Announcer, 1995
Treasurer, Glee Club, 1994 - 1995
Football Team, 1994 - 1996

REFERENCES

Provided on request.

LISA MOEN

1433 Eagleton Ave.
Charlotte, NC 19922
704/555-5565

JOB SOUGHT

A career in the field of nutrition.

EDUCATION

Charlotte College, Charlotte, NC
B.S. in Nutrition, expected May 1998

HONORS

Speilberg Nutrition Award
Dean's List, four semesters

EMPLOYMENT HISTORY

Charlotte Collge, Charlotte, NC
Assistant Nutritionist, 1996 to Present
Have planned over 250 menus with Head Nutritionist.
Oversee interviewing and hiring of student workers.

Angels Hospital, Brooklyn, NY
Assistant to Head Dietitian, Summers 1995 and 1996
Assisted with menus and meal planning.
Selected and delivered meals to special diet patients.

REFERENCES

Available upon request.

TREVOR MAINE
707 17th St.
Harrisburg, PA 39982
717/555-1689

EDUCATION

Pennsylvania State University, Harrisburg, PA
B.A. in Communications, expected June 1998
G.P.A. 3.36
Dean's List

COURSES

Journalism	Broadcasting
Mass Communications	Public Relations
Film	Child Psychology
Human Behavior	Sociology
English Literature	Child Welfare

WORK EXPERIENCE

Gamma Gamma Phi, Harrisburg, PA
Public Relations Assistant, 1996 - Present
Handle press releases and contacts with chapter members.
Help to establish new branch chapters.

HONORS

Panda Scholarship
Dean's List
Communications Honor Society
Gamma Gamma Phi

REFERENCES

Available on request

EUGENE T. SHOW

432 Sentinel Ave.
Kansas City, MO 74309
816/555-3903

OBJECTIVE:	A career in advertising media services.
EDUCATION:	STEVENS COLLEGE, Kansas City, MO
	B.A. in Advertising, expected June 1998
	3.66 G.P.A. in major field
	3.44 G.P.A. overall
	Student Government Secretary
	Homecoming Committee
	Plan to pursue a Master's degree at a future date.
WORK EXPERIENCE:	ANDERS PUBLISHING, INC., Kansas City, MO
	Marketing Intern, Summer 1997
	Assisted Marketing Manager of book publisher. Helped produce book catalog and develop pricing and marketing strategies. Tracked and analyzed sales of selected titles. Prepared sales analysis for management use.
	SURVEY SERVICE, INC., Kansas City, MO
	Telephone Surveyor. Summer 1995 and 1996
	RADICAL RECORDS, East Lydon, MO
	Salesperson, Summer 1994
SPECIAL SKILLS:	Working knowledge of German, French, and Spanish. Familiarity with WordPerfect and PageMaker programs. Typing speed of 65 w.p.m.

References Available

EUNICE T. HEYMAN
404 E. Peonia
Portland, ME 00088
207/555-5579

GOAL: A career in finance.

ACHIEVEMENTS

-Dispersed funds for student groups and activities.
-Designed operating budget for student government.
-Handled accounts payable and receivable.
-Approved financial reports.
-Served as co-chair of Budget Approval Committee.
-Oversaw deposits and withdrawals for customer accounts.
-Processed traveler's checks, cashier's checks, and money orders.

WORK
EXPERIENCE: FIRST BANK OF PORTLAND MAINE
                      Teller, June 1997 to Present

                      PORTLAND COLLEGE
                      Student Government Treasurer, September 1996 to June 1997

EDUCATION: Portland College, Portland, ME
                      B.S. in Business, June 1997
                      Minor in Accounting

REFERENCES: Available on request.

MICHELLE CRUMLEY
2316 SHERMAN AVE. #3B
EVANSTON, IL 60201

708/555-4727

EDUCATION: Northwestern University, Evanston, IL
                   B.S. in Journalism
                   Expected June 1998
                   G.P.A. of 3.6

HONORS: Phi Beta Kappa
                   Dean's List Seven Quarters
                   Owen L. Coon Award, Honorable Mention

ACTIVITIES: President, Activities and Organizations Board
                   Wa-Mu Show
                   Captain, Soccer Team
                   Freshman Advisor

WORK
EXPERIENCE: Evanston Review, Evanston, IL
                   Intern, Summer 1997
                   Assisted in layout, editing, and reporting for local newspaper.
                   Wrote and edited articles. Handled preparatory research for
                   local election coverage.

                   Northwestern University, Evanston, IL
                   General Office, Registrar, 1995 - 1997
                   Processed transcript requests. Entered registrations
                   on the computer. Provided information to students.

SPECIAL SKILLS: Knowledge of French & Russian.
                   Experience using WORDSTAR software.

REFERENCES: Available on request

MARGARET LEONARDO
Certified Legal Assistant

9991 E. Oak Drive 14C
Los Angles, CA 90029
213/555-1343

Education: California State University, Los Angeles, CA
Paralegal Program
Certificate of Completion, September 1997

University of California, Santa Barbara, CA
B.S. in English, May 1997
Summa Cum Laude

**Work
Experience:**   Oppenheim & Kensit, Los Angeles, CA
Intern 1/97 - 9/97
Drafted legal documents. Assisted in the preparation of cases for trial.
Conducted legal research. Handled memoranda of law.

Memberships: National Association of Legal Assistants

References: Provided on request

MICHELLE REIMER

7007 Catskills Ave #4　　　　　607/555-4444 (Home)
Ithaca, NY　　10299　　　　　607/555-2831 (Office)

OBJECTIVE:　　　Insurance Underwriter

EDUCATION:　　　ITHACA COLLEGE, Ithaca, NY
B.S. in Business Administration, May 1997
Minor in Spanish
Gergerheim Scholarship

Relevant Courses:

Principles of Insurance
Business Law
Tax Law
Business Risk Management
Accounting
Economics

**WORK
HISTORY:**　　　JOHNSON INSURANCE CO., Ithaca, NY
Junior Claims Representative, June 1997 - present
Process routine insurance claims. Flag questionable claims and conduct
preliminary investigation. Heavy phone contact with clients and health
care providers. Responsible for issuing monthly claims status report.

DAVIDSON & BROWNE, Attorneys at Law, Parker Meadows, NY
Legal Assistant, September 1995 to May 1997
Assisted attorneys part-time in handling insurance claims. Mastered legal
terms related to insurance work. Typing, filing, phones.

REFERENCES PROVIDED ON REQUEST

TIMOTHY WARSHAWSKI
555 Kenneth Ave.
Baltimore, MD 00029
301/555-7020

Goal: A career in the social service field.

Education: M.S.W., expected June 1998
                   University of Maryland, Baltimore, MD

                   B.A. in English, 1996
                   University of Georgia, Atlanta, GA

Coursework: Introduction to Psychology
                   Social Welfare Systems
                   Theory of Social Work
                   Abnormal Psychology
                   Urban Problems
                   Domestic Violence
                   History of Social Welfare
                   Business Management

Field Work: Counselor, 1997 to Present
                   Covenant House, Baltimore, MD

                   Interviewer, 1996 to 1997
                   Reach Drug Rehab Program, Baltimore, MD

                   Volunteer, 1995 to 1996
                   Baltimore Youth Center, Baltimore, MD

References: Available

AUDREY WEST
5968 Princeton Road
Las Vegas, NV 89890

720-555-6979

GOAL: Full-time position as magazine copy editor

EDUCATION: B.A. in English, June 1997
                   University of Southern California

SKILLS: Copyediting
                   Knowledge of Associated Press Style
                   Page Layout Experience
                   Photo Editing Experience
                   Familiar with QuarkXPress, PageMaker, Adobe
                       Photoshop and Adobe Illustrator

EXPERIENCE: Copy Editor, *Southwest Magazine*, 7/97 to Present

                   Copyedit features, check facts, prepare all material for
                   press. Assist in selection of photos and design of layouts.
                   Able to work in faced-paced atmosphere and meet tight
                   production deadlines.

                   Photo Editor, *USC News*, 9/96 to 6/97

                   Selected photos for alumni magazine, designed layout,
                   proofed copy.

REFERENCES: Available

ELIZABETH ENGLE
2316 King Street
Richardson, TX 75080
972/555-2552

GOAL

Petroleum engineering position with small, independent oil exploration and production company.

EDUCATION

University of Texas at Dallas
B.S. in Petroleum Engineering, expected May 1998

COURSEWORK

Petroleum Engineering Design
Rocks and Fluids
Reservoir Modeling
Reservoir Engineering
Secondary Recovery
Drilling Design & Production

WORK EXPERIENCE

UNIVERSITY OF TEXAS AT DALLAS
Lab Assistant/Physics Dept., 1996-1997

Assisted professors in the Physics Department with lab experiments and general office work.

MEMBERSHIPS

Society of Petroleum Engineers
Engineering Club

SPECIAL SKILLS

Working knowledge of Lotus 1-2-3 and Wordstar

REFERENCES AVAILABLE

Steven Ferris

589 Third Street
Bowling Green, KY 64490

502/555-4900 (Work)
502/555-3901 (Home)
Internet: sf@***.com**

EXPERTISE:	Corporate Identity Design Print Media Design Web Page Design
EDUCATION:	Colorado State University, Denver, CO Bachelor of Arts, June 1997 Major: Visual Communications Minor: Computer Science Knowledge of all major design software, including PageMaker, QuarkXPress, Adobe Illustrator, and Adobe Photoshop
WORK **EXPERIENCE:**	Colorado State University, Denver, CO Graphic Designer, University Publications Department July 1997 to Present Develop design concepts, page layouts, and cover designs for university publications including student yearbook, alumni directories, and academic journals. Extensive use of PageMaker and Adobe Illustrator programs.
MEMBERSHIPS:	Art Directors of Denver American Design Council Delta Gamma Fraternity
REFERENCES:	Provided upon request

DOUG WESTON

16 E. 3rd St.
Houston, TX 77702
713/555-5277

CAREER GOAL: To work as an attorney for a large law firm specializing in criminal law.

BAR
MEMBERSHIP: Texas State Bar, November 1997

EMPLOYMENT
EXPERIENCE:

Houston Public Defender's Office, Houston, TX
Law Clerk, 1996 to Present
Oversee minor crime investigations. Interview witnesses. Serve subpoenas.
Prepare investigation reports.

Nuhfer & Nuhfer, Houston, TX
Law Clerk, 1995 to 1996
Drafted pleadings. Performed field investigations. Researched case law.
Took depositions. Prepared trial briefs.

University of California, Irvine, CA
Student Assistant, Admissions Office, 1991 to 1994
Led campus tours for prospective students. Processed applications. Assisted
in student recruitment and general public relations activities.

EDUCATION:

Houston University, Houston, TX
Juris Doctor, May 1997
Class Rank: Top 10 percent

University of California, Irvine, CA
B.S. in Political Science, June 1993

HONORS:

Dean's List at Houston University, 1994 to 1997
Moot Court, National Competition
Texas Law Award

REFERENCES: Submitted upon request

David T. Sanchez
10001 W. Edina Ave.
Edina, MN 53989
612/555-5453

STRENGTHS:

- Excellent communication and people skills
- Strong photographic and processing skills
- Academic and hands-on training in commercial art
- Computer literate, with working knowledge of QuarkXPress and PageMaker

EDUCATION:

University of Minnesota, St. Paul, MN
B.A. in Commercial Art, expected May 1998

WORK EXPERIENCE:

Minneapolis Magazine, Minneapolis, MN
Commercial Artist, Summers 1995 - present

University of Minnesota, St. Paul, MN
Designer, University Publications, 1997

University of Minnesota, St. Paul, MN
Photographer, Student Gazette, 1996-1997

WORKSHOPS:

Website Design Seminar, University of Minnesota, 1997
Illustration Workshop, Art Institute of Chicago, 1996
Midwest Design Seminar, Northern Illinois University, 1995

REFERENCES AVAILABLE

STEWART KENNETH CAHL, C.L.A.
4201 N. Broadway
Lafayette, IN 47906

317/555-7498 (Office)
317/555-6968 (Home)
skc@***.netcom.com (E-mail)

OVERVIEW

Graduate of paralegal training program at Roosevelt University, ranked in top 10 percent of class. Received C.L.A. certification from National Association of Legal Assistants. Currently employed by small legal firm specializing in tax and corporate law. Seeking to use my skills in legal research and document preparation at large law firm where I may broaden my exposure to all areas of the law.

EXPERIENCE

- Draft legal documents
- Conduct legal research
- Attend hearings
- Handle SEC filings
- Compile case citations
- Assist in preparing witnesses for depositions
- Prepare cases for appeals

EMPLOYERS

SIMON, ROBB & HOBBES, Lafayette, IN
Legal Assistant, July 1997 - present

COHEN & COHEN, Raleigh, NC
Office Assistant, May 1996 to June 1997

EDUCATION

ROOSEVELT UNIVERSITY, Chicago, IL : Paralegal Training Program
Certificate, June 1997

NORTH CAROLINA STATE UNIVERSITY, Raleigh, NC: B.A. in Economics,
June 1996

KEVIN WONG

5449 Magnolia Way #4B
North Hollywood, CA
818/555-7344

OBJECTIVE

Production Assistant

WORK EXPERIENCE

SABER PRODUCTIONS, Burbank, CA
Production Assistant, June 1997 - present
Assisted television producer and production coordinator. Organized transportation for cast and crew members. Copied and distributed scripts. Assisted location manager.

FEDER FILM PRODUCTIONS, San Francisco, CA
Production Coordinator, Summer 1996
Scouted locations; acquired film permits and props. Handled airline reservations and accommodations for talent. Oversaw the distribution of press releases. Photographed promotional stills. Supervised extras.

CHICAGO FILM FESTIVAL, Chicago, IL
Production Assistant, Summer 1995
Helped produce and distribute promotional material. Assisted with the day-to-day operations of the film festival.

KBT RADIO, University of Seattle, Seattle, WA
Producer, 1995 - 1997
Served as an announcer on a weekly newscast. Edited copy for newscast. Investigated and reported on student events. Handled on-air coverage of local elections. Trained and supervised new employees.

EDUCATION

UNIVERSITY OF SEATTLE, Seattle, WA
B.A. in Film Production, June 1997

REFERENCES PROVIDED UPON REQUEST

CLARENCE SCOTT TALLEY
600 W. Porter St.
Las Vegas, NV 89890
702/555-3893

EDUCATION

University of Nevada, Las Vegas, NV
Bachelor of Arts in Communications
Expected June 1998

HONORS

Dean's List (four semesters)
Dornburn Academic Merit Scholarship
U.N.L.V. Communications Award (given to outstanding student researcher)

ACTIVITIES

President, Kappa Beta Fraternity
New Student Week Committee
Homecoming Planning Committee
Captain, Tennis Team

WORK EXPERIENCE

Porter Rand & Associates, Seattle, WA
Advertising Intern, 1997
Assisted sales staff in the areas of
research,
demographics,
sales forecasts,
identifying new customers,
and promotion.

University of Nevada, Las Vegas, NV
Research/Office Assistant, 1996-1997
Researched and compiled materials for department professors.
Arranged filing system and supervisor's library.
Organized department inventory.

DAN LUI

17 Dinge Road
Terre Haute, IN 52211
317/555-1331(Home)
317/555-2339 (Office)

OBJECTIVE: A position in the field of Electrical Engineering with an emphasis on aviation electronic systems.

EDUCATION: B.S. in Electrical Engineering, May 1997
Rose-Hulman Institute of Technology, Terre Haute, IN
G.P.A. 3.75
Graduated with Honors

**WORK
EXPERIENCE:**   C & S Industrial Design Consultants, Richardson, TX
Summer Intern, 1996
Assisted in research and development department of
aviation electronics firm. Input data, typed performance specifications
reports, calibrated lasers, and maintained test equipment.

Rose-Hulman Institute of Technology, Terre Haute, IN
Assistant to the Director, Financial Aid, 1995-1996
Processed applications. Handled general office duties.

ACTIVITIES: President of Student Chapter of Institute of Electrical and Electronics
Engineers
Peer Advisor, Engineering Department

REFERENCES: Available upon request

PATRICIA YOUNG
66 Chambers Road
Hartford, CT 00112
203/555-2229

OVERVIEW: Seeking position as English Teacher at the Secondary School level.
Currently completing M.A. thesis project.
Provisionally licensed to teach in the State of Connecticut.

EDUCATION: UNIVERSITY OF HARTFORD, West Hartford, CT
Master's Degree in Education, expected June 1998
G.P.A. of 4.0 in major

GRINNELL COLLEGE, Grinnell, IA
Bachelor's Degree in Education, with a minor in English

EXPERIENCE: CENTRAL HIGH SCHOOL, Hartford, CT
Student Teacher, English Department
January 1998 - Present
Supervisor: Kaye Brendt

UNIVERSITY OF HARTFORD, West Hartford, CT
Tutor, Writing Lab
September 1997 - December 1997

GRINNELL COLLEGE, Grinnell, IA
Teaching Assistant for Expository Writing Course

MEMBERSHIPS: American Federation of Teachers
National Education Association

REFERENCES: Submitted upon request.

Qeeri Tujamota

1290 W. Forest Avenue
Milwaukee, WI 55409

414/555-2029
tujamota@technoserve.comm
www/http.tujamota

GRAPHIC DESIGNER

EXPERIENCE:

Regis Advertising, Milwaukee, WI
Graphic Designer, 1996 to Present
Handle development and execution of projects from initial design through completion of camera-ready art.

University of Illinois, Chicago, IL
Graphic Designer, University Art Gallery, 1995-1996
Designed posters and brochures to promote student art exhibits.

University of Illinois, Chicago, IL
Graphic Designer, Media Center, 1994-1995
Assisted faculty and staff with design concepts. Helped produce camera-ready art for special events, curriculum support, and distance learning projects.

EDUCATION:

University of Illinois, Chicago, IL
B.A. in Visual Communications, 1996

MEMBERSHIPS:

Midwest Design Coalition
Women in Design

AWARDS:

Midwest Design Coalition's Contest for Advertising Design, Honorable Mention, October 1997

University of Illinois Art Show, Best in Show, June 1996

REFERENCES:

References and portfolio provided upon request.

GEORGE PASTERNECK

1119 S. Figueroa Ave.
Miami, FL 33303
305/555-6766

EDUCATION

University of Miami, Miami, FL
Graduate School of Business Administration
M.B.A. expected, June 1998
Concentration: Finance
Finance Club
Student Advisory Board

Boston University, Boston, MA
B.A. in Economics, 1996
Summa Cum Laude
Phi Beta Kappa
Student Government Vice-President

WORK EXPERIENCE

Studebaker & Bostwick, Miami, FL
Financial Accounting Intern, 9/97 to Present
Participate in standard accounting, credit approval, budgeting, and variance analysis. Handle
bank balances and money management.

First Florida Bank, Ft. Lauderdale, FL
Commercial Loan Intern, 1/97 to 5/97
Oversaw accounts in the automated teller system. Provided financial data to commercial account
officers. Handled the collection of arrears.

Boston University, Boston, MA
Assistant, Accounts Payable Department, 9/95 to 12/97
Assisted with bookkeeping, check requests, and disbursements. Billed invoices. Tracked accounts
receivable and accounts payable.

REFERENCES

Available upon request

James Thornborough Newton

1171 Davis St. #2
Evanston, IL 60202
847-555-2741

Objective:

Staff Writer/Researcher for a news department of a newspaper where I can use my editorial, writing, and reporting skills.

Education:

NORTHWESTERN UNIVERSITY, Evanston, IL
B.A. in Journalism & Political Science (Double Major)
Expected Graduation Date: June 1998

Accomplishments:

--Write regular column on political issues for campus newspaper.

--Won journalism award for feature series on "The Nuclear Threat."

--Researched and wrote pamphlets for city council on crime, gentrification, and zoning.

--Edited grant proposals for local theater company.

--Served as assistant researcher for NBC opinion poll.

Employment History:

THE DAILY NORTHWESTERN, Evanston, IL
STAFF WRITER, 1995 to Present

EVANSTON CITY COUNCIL, Evanston, IL
RESEARCHER/WRITER, 1996 to 1997

VICTORY GARDENS THEATER, Chicago, IL
EDITOR, 1996

NBC-TV, Chicago, IL
RESEARCHER, 1996

References:

Available on request

PATRICIA TYRONE

1600 Holiday Drive #4   209/555-4444
Modesto, CA 95350   209/555-2831

OBJECTIVE: Position as an underwriter for an insurance company.

EDUCATION: UNIVERSITY OF CALIFORNIA, Davis, CA
                        B.S. in Business Administration, 1996
                        Minor in Spanish
                        Gergerheim Academic Merit Scholarship

                        Major Courses:

                        Principles of Insurance
                        Business Law
                        Tax Law
                        Business Risk Management
                        Accounting
                        Economics

**WORK
HISTORY:**   HAMILTON INSURANCE CO., Davis, CA
                        Junior Claims Representative, 1996 - present
                        Evaluate and process claims. Advanced to handling claims after an
                        eight-week training period.

                        PATTERSON & WAKEFIELD, Attorneys at Law, Emoryville, CA
                        Legal Assistant, 1995-1996
                        Assisted attorneys part-time in handling insurance claims. Mastered
                        legal terms related to insurance work. Typing, filing, phones.

                        REFERENCES PROVIDED ON REQUEST

JENRETTE ALANA UPJOHN

8970 E. University Drive #1
Phoenix, AZ 78870
602/555-2922 (Home)
602/555-4000 (Office)

OBJECTIVE: A career in radio.

SKILLS AND ACCOMPLISHMENTS:

- Assisted in the management of a college radio station.
- Helped to direct and supervise staff.
- Established music format guidelines.
- Wrote and edited budget proposals.
- Assisted in financial matters.
- Created and implemented new music format.
- Arranged station-sponsored performances of local artists.
- Served as on-air personality.
- Trained a staff of disc jockeys.

EMPLOYMENT HISTORY:

WPHO-FM, Phoenix, AZ
Assistant General Manager, 1997 to Present

WTTW-TV, Chicago, IL
Intern, 1996

WTTO-RADIO, Toluca, AZ
Music Director, Summer 1995

EDUCATION:

UNIVERSITY OF ARIZONA, Phoenix, AZ
B.A. in Broadcasting,
Degree expected in June 1998

References provided on request.

GREG GOLD
1661 Corn Row Drive
Cedar Rapids, IA 53309

319/555-2909 (Home)
319/555-8888 (Work)

JOB OBJECTIVE: Engineering Technician/Camera Operator

OVERVIEW: Experience with all camera operations for film and video. Skills include studio lighting, set design, film editing, dubbing, gaffing, audio-video switching, mixing, and technical troubleshooting.

EXPERIENCE: WCED-TV, Cedar Rapids, IA
Engineering Assistant, 7/96 - present

Drawbridge Productions, Des Moines, IA
Assistant Camera Operator, Summer 1995

WWOR Radio, Jackson, MS
Engineer, 9/94 - 6/95

EDUCATION: Jackson University, Jackson, MS
B.A. in Communication Arts, June 1996

REFERENCES: Available on request.

KEVIN B. LANCE

202 W. Slade Street
Duluth, MN 56690
218/555-7779

JOB SOUGHT: Credit Clerk for a large retail chain.

EXPERIENCE:

Duluth College, Duluth, MN
Student Government Treasurer, 1996 to Present

Disperse funds for student groups and activities. Design operating budget for student government. Handle accounts payable and receivable. Approve financial reports. Serve as co-chair of Budget Approval Committee.

First Bank of Duluth, Duluth, MN
Teller, 1994 to 1996

Oversaw deposits and withdrawals for customer accounts. Processed traveler's checks, cashier's checks, and money orders.

EDUCATION:

Duluth College, Duluth, MN
B.S. in Business, expected June 1997
Minor in Accounting

REFERENCES: Available on request

TYRELL STEVENSON
602 S. TEXAS AVE.
OAKLAND, CA 99999

415/555-3168

JOB OBJECTIVE:

A position in hotel management.

EDUCATION:

International School of Business, San Francisco, CA
1/96 - present
Major: Hotel Management

World Travel Institute, Sacramento, CA
1994
Certificate, Travel Consultant

Eastern Illinois University, Alton, IL
Attended 1990-1992
Area of concentration: Business Management

WORK EXPERIENCE:

Reddraan, Inc., Oakland, CA
Manager/Sales Executive, 11/95 - present

Manager/sales executive for cookware business. Sell cookware at wholesale and
retail levels. Negotiate prices with customers. Handle all finances and bookkeeping.

Eastmont Hotel, Oakland, CA
Student Intern, 1/97 - 6/97

Assisted food and beverage manager for 200-key hotel. Responsibilities included
inventory management, data entry, and purchasing duties.

Westerly Travel, Chicago, IL
Travel Consultant, 6/94 - 12/96

Sold airline tickets and tour packages. Advised customers on travel plans. Handled ARC
reports to airline corporations.

References available on request.

Chapter Six

SAMPLE COVER LETTERS

DAN LUI

17 Dinge Road
Terre Haute, IN 52211
317/555-1331
317/555-2339

August 21, 19--

Farrallon, Inc.
787 E. Fourier Drive
Emeryville, CA 96998

Attn: Robert Crain, Director of Human Services

Dear Mr. Crain:

After your visit to Rose-Hulman last March, we spoke about opportunities within your company for electrical engineers. You indicated that new positions would be opening this fall. I am writing to request an interview for one of those openings.

In May, I graduated from Rose-Hulman with a B.S. in Electrical Engineering. I was one of fifteen out of two hundred who graduated with honors. My coursework included microwave circuit design, electromagnetic waves, digital integrated circuits, and systems and signals.

As I look forward to my career in this field, I know that I would be able to make good use of my education working for Farrallon.

I have enclosed a copy of my resume and will call next week to discuss setting up an interview.

Sincerely,

Dan Lui

June 1, 19--

Ed Peters
Principal
East Ridge High School
7001 Woodridge Rd.
Hartford, CT 00122

Dear Mr. Peters:

I am responding to your advertisement in the *Hartford Gazette* for a Spanish teacher. As the enclosed resume indicates, I have the credentials you are seeking, and I am eager to put my skills to work for East Ridge.

My background includes a B.A. in Secondary Education from Hartford College with a minor in Spanish. My student teaching experience includes two semesters teaching Spanish I and one semester supervising a discussion section of Spanish Literature at Central High School.

I would enjoy hearing more about the current opening and hope that you will call me at 203-555-2229 to discuss the matter further. It is easiest to reach me in the morning, between 8 and 10 a.m.

Thank you in advance for your time and consideration.

Sincerely,

Patricia Young
66 Chambers Road
Hartford, CT 00112

August 8, 19--

Tika Woods
Director of Personnel
Department of Children's Services
City of Oakland
33 W. 43rd Street
Oakland, CA 94990

Dear Ms. Woods:

As a recent graduate of Stanford University' s Master of Social Work program, I am looking forward to a rewarding career as a provider of social services to disadvantaged children. As an Oakland native, I feel a special affinity to this city and a unique desire to help make it a better place for our children to live. For these reasons, I am writing to find out if you have openings for a Children's Caseworker.

While at Stanford, my studies included Theory of Social Work, Urban Problems, Case Analysis, Abnormal Psychology, and Social Welfare Systems, among others. My field work includes positions as a counselor for Covenant House in Oakland, as an interviewer for the Oakland Drug Rehab Program, and as a volunteer for the San Francisco Youth Center.

I feel that my training and experience in the field well qualify me for a position in your agency. Please contact me if you would like me to come in for an interview.

Sincerely,

John Marum
489 McCauley
Oakland, CA 94609
415/555-7020

Terri Franks
15 Nob Hill
San Francisco, CA 91405
415/555-4398

January 3, 19--

Gilbert Secor, President
Unicorn Design, Inc.
2442 Market St., Suite 4C
San Francisco, CA   91407

Dear Mr. Secor:

Your art director, Robin White, recently informed me that Unicorn Designs is interested in hiring additional graphic designers. I'm writing to introduce myself and to let you know of my interest in working for your firm as a graphic designer.

As the enclosed resume indicates, I am a recent graduate of the Berkeley College of Design where I received a B.A. in Graphic Design. My areas of concentration included photography, publication design, copywriting, typography, and packaging. I also earned a B.A. in History from the University of Minnesota in 1992.

My design experience includes the designing of ads, brochures, and posters, coordinating of fashion shows, and creating business systems. I have worked as a graphic design intern at Berkeley and as a graphics assistant at Fern Labs.

Now that I have earned my degree and gained the needed experience, I am ready for the challenge of a position at a company such as yours.

I would like to show you my portfolio. Please feel free to call me for an interview at your convenience.

Sincerely,

Terri Franks

October 3, 19--

Fernetta Hippleman
Head Librarian
Seattle Public Library
5000 Lake Parkway
Seattle, WA 98888

Dear Ms. Hippleman:

I am applying for the position of Reference Librarian which you posted in the
Library Science Department at the University of Oregon.

I am attending the University of Oregon's Library Science program and expect to
be graduated in June of 1998. I earned my undergraduate degree, a B.S. in Linguistics,
from the University of Mississippi.

While attending school at the University of Oregon, I have interned at the Eugene
Public Library. I've also assisted the children's librarian at the Oxford Public Library.

The enclosed resume should help you evaluate my qualifications. I look forward
to meeting you and discussing this position in the near future.

Sincerely,

Carol Page
5000 E. Maple St.
Apartment 4
Eugene, OR 97412
503/555-4122

May 15, 19--

Deborah Klugh
Director of Human Resources
ABC
11 Rockefeller Plaza
New York, NY 10019

Dear Ms. Klugh:

This letter is in response to your ad in <u>The New York Times</u> for a P.R. assistant. Enclosed are my resume and salary requirements as requested in the ad.

Next month I will be graduating from Boston University with a degree in Communications and a concentration in Public Relations. I was inducted into Phi Beta Kappa this month and expect to graduate with honors in June.

I am interested in working in the television industry and would be most pleased to be a part of the ABC team. I possess strong written and verbal communication skills and feel certain that I would do an excellent job in meeting the demands of this position.

Please contact me if you are interested. I am willing to travel to New York for an interview if necessary. Thank you for your time and consideration.

Sincerely,

Barton T. Quigley
Boston University
Fenton Hall
199 W. Hampshire Way
Boston, MA 02201
617/555-3839

April 23, 19--

Harvard Peter Fendi
President
American Finance Co.
4444 E. River Drive
Detroit, MI 33393

Dear Mr. Fendi:

As a recent graduate of The Kellogg School of Business Management at Northwestern University, I am seeking a position in financial management. I met a representative of your company, Jonathan Siveva, at a recruiting seminar at Northwestern a few months ago and he alerted me to the fact that your company would be hiring M.B.A.s this summer. Hence, this letter.

At Kellogg, my concentration was in finance, and I was in the Finance Club and served as a member of the Student Advisory Board. My practical experience includes a financial accounting internship at Thomas & Thomas, an internship in the commercial loan department at LaSalle National Bank, and a position in the accounts payable department at Northwestern.

I am enclosing my resume for a more comprehensive picture of my accomplishments and qualifications. I will contact you in the next ten days to inquire about setting up an interview.

Sincerely,

Antonio Marino
8900 Lake Shore Drive #442
Chicago, IL 60614
312/555-2939

July 22, 19--

Neil Tennant
Director of Human Resources
Parker Thomas Accounting, Inc.
7717 E. 3rd Terrace
Milwaukee, WI 55250

Dear Mr. Tennant:

I am seeking employment in the field of accounting, particularly a position that might prepare me for management.

I am a recent M.B.A. graduate of the University of Wisconsin at Madison. My area of concentration at the University was accounting, and my courses included the following:

Basic, Intermediate, and Advanced Accounting
Business Law
Cost Accounting
Statistical Methods
Planning and Control
Tax Law
Investments

Prior to my graduate degree, I earned a B.A. in History from the University of Chicago where I won the Leopold Scholarship, which is given to an outstanding senior by the History Department.

The enclosed resume provides further details about my preparation for an accounting career. I would also welcome the opportunity to present my qualifications in person and to learn more about your current needs in the area of accounting. I will call early next week regarding possible job openings. Thank you for your time and consideration.

Sincerely,

William Gavin
2666 Western Ave. #44
Madison, WI 55590
414/555-2029

December 13, 19--

Hollywood Reporter
Box 1140-H
465 Hollywood Way
Burbank, CA 91505

I am responding to your ad in last week's edition for a public relations assistant at a major Hollywood production company. I am enclosing my resume and salary requirements as requested.

I am a recent graduate of California State University at Northridge where I received a B.A. in Communications. My work includes an internship at Warner Bros. Studios in Burbank in the public relations department. My goal is a career in public relations in the entertainment industry.

I am anxious to learn more about this position and look forward to hearing from you soon. Please feel free to call me at home or at work. Thank you for your time and consideration.

Sincerely,

Ken Phillips
4000 Sunset Blvd.
Los Angeles, CA 90028

213/555-7648 (Home)
213/555-2000 (Work)

February 18, 19--

Richard Marx
Manager
Westin Hotel
1131 6th St.
Seattle, WA 98802

Dear Mr. Marx:

I am looking to break into the hotel business with a long-term goal of management. I am forwarding my resume to you with the hope that you may have an opening on your staff.

My credentials for such a position include the education I have received at the International School of Business in San Francisco. I recently graduated with a Certificate in Hotel Management. While still in school, I completed an internship at the Eastmont Hotel, assisting the Food and Beverage Manager.

My previous work experience includes management of my own cookware business and employment as a travel consultant. In each of these positions my supervisors and business associates have praised me for being reliable, hard-working, and competent.

Thank you for taking the time to review my qualifications. I am available at your convenience if you wish to schedule an interview.

Sincerely,

Tyrell Stevenson
602 S. Texas Ave.
Oakland, CA 99999
415/555-3168

Martha Wayans
4500 77th Street
New York, NY 10032
212/555-3839

August 28, 19--

George Jacobs
Human Resources
AT&T
1200 E. 5th Ave.
New York, NY 10019

Dear Mr. Jacobs:

Mitchell Sanderson, who works the sales department at AT&T, suggested that I contact you regarding a possible opening in your public relations department. I am enclosing my resume for your consideration.

I will be graduating this month from New York University with a degree in Communications. My recent induction into the Communications Honor Society (Beta Alpha Psi) was a personal milestone. I am also a member of the Association of International Business (A.I.B.).

I am interested in working in the communications industry in the field of public relations and I feel that the best place for me to start would be at AT&T.

I will be calling you in about a week to follow up on this letter. Please feel free to call Mr. Sanderson for a reference.

Sincerely,

Martha Wayans

January 28, 19--

Helena Borgess
Director of Human Resources
Warner Bros., Inc.
4000 Olive Ave.
Burbank, CA 91505

Dear Ms. Borgess:

I am writing to inquire about openings in your company in the area of Human Resources. My area of interest is the entertainment industry, and that is why I am writing to you.

I will be graduating from UCLA with a degree in Business in June of this year. Human Resources has been an area of focus in my studies. Last summer, I served as an intern in the Human Resources department at TPT, Inc. in Burbank where I assisted with personnel acquisition and evaluation. My specific duties included administering tests to prospective employees and setting up appointments for interviews.

The enclosed resume provides further details about my qualifications. If it interests you, I would be happy to interview with you at your convenience.

Sincerely,

Reva Poperman
UCLA
Snadler Hall
144 Glendon Ave.
Los Angeles, CA 90289
213/555-2384

February 12, 19--

Wendell C. Wilkerson
Editor
Richmond Register
330 S. Potomac Drive
Richmond, VA 11980

Dear Mr. Wilkerson:

I am writing in response to your opening for a beat reporter which
was posted at the career office at the University of Virginia.
I am currently seeking a position in the field of journalism and
wish to be considered for this opening.

I will graduate this June with a B.A. in Journalism from the
University of Virginia. My writing/reporting experience includes
a stint as Senior Editor of the campus newspaper, editing of a
literary magazine, and a broadcast journalism internship with
WRCH-TV, all right here in Richmond.

My enclosed resume details my experience. I am available for an
interview at your convenience.

Thank you for considering me.

Sincerely,

Samuel Travis Shavers
15 E. Greenview St. #333
Richmond, VA 18978
804/555-3903

November 1, 19--

Peter Sauers
Managing Director
Sauers Productions, Inc.
550 Magnolia Way
Burbank, CA 91501

Dear Mr Sauers:

Are you in need of a dedicated, energetic, and resourceful production assistant?

I have spent the last year working in Miami for New Order Productions as a production assistant. I have benefited greatly from this experience, but it has always been my dream to work in the Hollywood film industry. Hence, this letter. Last summer, I served as production coordinator for Tert Films in Chicago, and the summer before I was production assistant for the Baltimore Film Festival. I received a B.A. in Film Production from the University of Florida in 1996.

Sauers Productions does quality work, and I would be pleased to contribute as a new member of your staff.

I hope the enclosed resume interests you. I will follow this letter with a phone call next week.

Sincerely,

Milton Carl Chapman
66446 Collins Ave. #4B
Miami, FL 30309
305/555-2930
305/555-2992

May 17, 19--

David D. Geras
Director of Broadcast Operations
WGN-TV
700 W. Addison
Chicago, IL 60625

Dear Mr. Geras:

I enjoyed meeting and speaking with you at the Broadcast Careers seminar at Howard University last spring. I am writing to you now to express my interest in an opening at WGN for a News Assistant. I am enclosing my resume for your review.

Besides the B.A. degree in Journalism which I will receive next month, I have gained experience over the last four summers in a variety of workplaces. Most recently, I completed an internship at WDC-TV in Washington, DC, where I assisted in the production of a news show. Previous internships include <u>Capitol Magazine</u>, <u>Chattanooga News</u>, and Park Advertising, Inc.

I would be glad to come to Chicago for an interview at your convenience. Thank you for your time and consideration.

Sincerely,

Terri Bakkemo
700 Thornborough Rd.
Chattanooga, TN 75221
615/555-2111

April 23, 1991

Rupert Goebert
Director
Santa Barbara Art Fair
6660 Forest Green Ave.
Santa Barbara, CA 92299

Dear Mr. Goebert:

I am interested in applying for the position of photographer for
this year's Santa Barbara Art Fair. I learned of the position
from your posting at the civic center.

My photography experience includes a stint as official
photographer for the Nevada State Fair last year where I headed
a team of photographers. I have worked with 35mm and
2 1/4 x 2 1/4-inch cameras along with video equipment. I have
photographed for products, promotions, press releases, and
publications. I believe that my background has prepared me to
do an excellent job for you.

I am a graduate of the University of Washington in Tacoma
where I earned a degree in Graphic Arts with a minor in
Photography. I also have experience as a graphic designer.

My resume is enclosed, along with a few samples of my
photography. I will be in touch with you next week regarding
this letter. I appreciate your consideration.

Sincerely,

Peter Klept
554 Grambling Road
Santa Barbara, CA 97770
815/555-2332

August 23, 19--

David Bascombe III
Sears & Roebuck, Inc.
1000 S. Adams
Chicago, IL 60601

Dear Mr. Bascombe:

I am responding to your job listing for a Marketing Management Trainee which was posted in the placement office at Boston University. I am interested in applying for this position and am enclosing my resume with this letter.

I have recently graduated from Boston University with a degree in Economics, and I am anxious to find employment in the marketing field. I am willing to relocate for the right position.

My work experience includes employment as a Marketing Assistant for Lewis Advertising Agency in Boston and as a Telephone Surveyor for Paterno Marketing.

I will be in the Chicago area the week of 9/12. Would it be possible to set up an interview with you during that week? If so, please contact me at your earliest convenience.

Sincerely,

Janis Darien
345 W. 3rd. St., Apt. 42
Boston, MA 02210
617/555-3291

CLARENCE SCOTT TALLEY III
600 Porter Street
Las Vegas, NV 89890

702-555-3893

May 15, 19--

Mr. Tarskett Renu
Creative Director
Quest Advertising
2330 W. Delaney Blvd.
Los Angeles, CA 90029

Dear Mr. Renu:

This is a letter of inquiry. I am curious to know whether there are any openings in your agency at the present time.

I expect to graduate next month from the University of Nevada with a B.A. in Communications, and I am looking toward a career in advertising. While at Nevada, I was awarded the Dornburn Scholarship and a Communications Award. I also made the Dean's List four times.

Last summer, I gained experience in the field by serving as an advertising intern for Porter and Rand Associates. There I assisted the sales staff in the areas of research, demographics, sales forecasts, and special promotions. The experience gained in this internship, along with my education, have given a good foundation to begin my career in advertising.

I would appreciate hearing of any current openings at Quest, and am willing to travel to Los Angeles at your convenience to discuss opportunities in person. Thank you.

Sincerely,

Clarence Scott Talley III

THEORDORE L. MCDONALD

2107 Adams St. #9
Austin, TX 78711
512/55S-7665

December 8, 19--

Austin Hospital
444 E. Grand Ave.
Austin, TX 78712
Attn: Melissa Ward
          Human Resources

Dear Ms. Ward:

This letter is in response to your ad in the *Austin Times* for a dietitian for the children's wing of your hospital. I am enclosing my resume for your consideration in light of this opening.

The position interests me both because it matches my qualifications and because I have worked for Austin Hospital before. I gained valuable experience during the summers assisting your head dietitian with menus and meal planning. My first full-time job, as assistant nutritionist at the University of Texas, has been a challenge. I've helped to plan over 250 menus as well as overseeing the interviewing and hiring of student workers.

I am a recent graduate of the University of Texas where I received a B.S. in Nutrition. While at the university, I received the Speilberg Nutrition Award and earned a spot on the Dean' s List four different semesters.

The current opening at Austin Hospital sounds like a challenging one, and I feel that I am up to the challenge. I look forward to hearing from you regarding this opportunity.

Sincerely,

Theodore L. McDonald

May 24, 19--

John D. Peck
Peck, Sylbert & Peck
55 E. Monroe St.
Toronto, Ontario, Canada M6P 4C7

Dear Mr. Peck:

Professor Gerald Stevens at the Toronto School of Law asked me to write to you to inquire about an opening at your law firm. I will be graduating from the Toronto School next month with a Juris Doctor degree and a concentration in legal medicine. It is my desire to remain in the Toronto area after graduation, and Professor Stevens recommends your firm highly.

Currently, I am interning at Tannen & Hope here in Toronto where I draft legal documents, assist in trial preparation, and conduct legal research. I feel this internship has been a valuable experience for me and has helped to prepare me for a career as an attorney.

My resume is enclosed for your review. I appreciate your consideration and will check with you next week regarding an interview.

Sincerely,

Christine Harding
3333 N. Halen Ave. #3B
Toronto, Ontario, Canada M6P 4C7
416/555-2333